SPAIN

TITLES IN THE MODERN NATIONS OF THE WORLD SERIES INCLUDE:

Brazil
Canada
China
Cuba
Egypt
England
Germany
Greece
India
Ireland
Italy
Japan
Kenya
Mexico
Russia
Somalia
South Africa
South Korea
Spain
Sweden
The United States

SPAIN

BY JOHN F. GRABOWSKI

LUCENT BOOKS
P.O. BOX 289011
SAN DIEGO, CA 92198-9011

Library of Congress Cataloging-in-Publication Data

Grabowski, John F.
   Spain / John F. Grabowski.
      p.   cm. — (Modern nations of the world)
   Includes bibliographical references and index.
   Summary: Examines the land, people, and history of Spain and
discusses its current state of affairs and place in the world today.
   ISBN 1-56006-602-4 (lib. : alk. paper)
   1. Spain   [1. Spain.] I. Title.   II. Series.
DP17.G73 2000
946—dc21   99-33516
                                                                   CIP

Copyright © 2000 by Lucent Books, Inc.
P.O. Box 289011, San Diego, CA 92198-9011
Printed in the U.S.A.

CONTENTS

INTRODUCTION

A LAND OF CONTRASTS

A person examining a map of Spain might well get the impression of a relatively compact country of comparatively uniform features. Bordered as it is by the rugged Pyrenees in the northeast and water everywhere else, the Iberian Peninsula—consisting of Spain and Portugal—appears almost as an island. Technically a part of Europe, Spain in many respects has closer ties to Africa. The narrow strait that separates the country from the northern part of the African continent was a far less impressive barrier to invading armies than were the mountains to the north, which isolated the inhabitants from the rest of Europe. One might predict the development of a homogeneous, somewhat insular culture in such a region.

Closer examination, however, reveals an entirely different story. The image of geographic unity is more illusion than reality. The high tablelands that compose the greater part of the landmass are separated into distinct regions by a jumble of crisscrossing chains of mountains. With such buffers as a deterrent to communication and transportation, separate regional identities developed among native groups. In addition to geographical distinctions are differences in climate, culture, and, most importantly, language. Indeed, even today, many Spaniards express loyalty to their *patria chica*, or small homeland, rather than to Spain as a nation.

THE SPANISH CHARACTER

A further obstacle hindering the formation of a single unified people is the nature of the essential Spanish personality. Historically, the Spaniard has been a fiercely independent person who displays a tenacious, powerful will. His intense pride and personal dignity show through in his individual achievements, both triumphs and failures. "The Spaniard," writes Dr. John A. Crow, an authority on Hispanic culture, ". . . does not feel that he is born to realize any social end, but that he is born primarily to realize himself. His sense of personal dignity is admirable at times, exasperating at others; selfhood is the center of his gravity."[1]

A resolute disposition is a requirement for survival in Spain's often adverse, unforgiving environment. It is revealed in the individualism of the conquistadores of the sixteenth century who helped establish Spain as a major world power. Spanish adventurers and explorers exhibited this ambition and willpower, and these qualities have been displayed, likewise, by the Spanish artists, writers, and musicians who have graced the world with their creative inspirations.

At the same time, however, the individual must be willing to surrender a measure of his independence in order to work

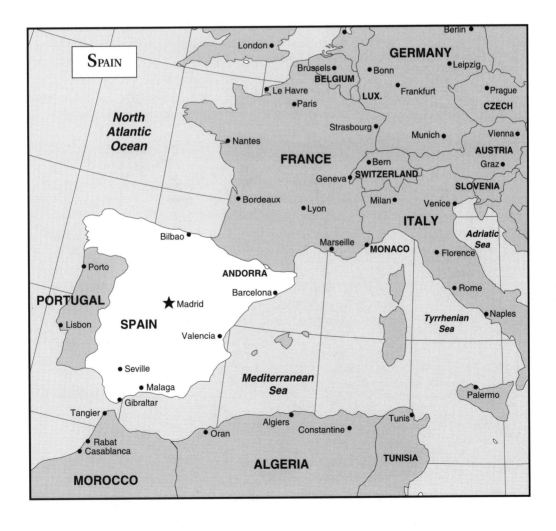

with others in the common interest. This is difficult for a Galician to do, for example, if he considers himself a Galician first and a Spaniard second. It is an even more formidable task when the Galician speaks a different language than the Catalan or the Castilian or the Basque.

Tempering traditional individualism in the national interest is the challenge faced by the modern-day people of Spain. The patchwork of cultures that is Spain must attempt to come to terms with its diversity and blend together to present a united front to the world at large. What it means to be Spanish is changing. To understand these changes, we must examine the country, its history, and its people.

EMERGENCE OF A WORLD POWER

The Kingdom of Spain—*Reino de España* in Spanish—occupies nearly 85 percent of the Iberian Peninsula in the southwestern corner of Europe. With a total area of almost 195,000 square miles, it is the third-largest country in Europe, after Ukraine and France; with a population just under 40 million, its population density of approximately 205 people per square mile is lower than that of most European nations.

Spain's elevation is one of the highest in western Europe, second only to Switzerland's. It is bordered by the Bay of Biscay to the northwest, France and Andorra to the northeast, the Mediterranean Sea to the southeast and east, the Strait of Gibraltar to the south, and the Atlantic Ocean and Portugal to the west. Its strategic location—separating the rest of mainland Europe from Africa and the Atlantic Ocean from the Mediterranean Sea—and reports of great mineral wealth have drawn Spain to the attention of peoples from the surrounding regions over the centuries. To understand how its turbulent history has shaped the personality of the modern-day nation, one must examine the composition of the land, since geographical features play an important role in the pattern of historical development.

MAINLAND SPAIN

Spain is a country of both beauty and contrast. The land itself may be divided into five principal geographic regions. Administratively, these regions make up seventeen political districts, known as autonomous communities. These communities, which vary greatly in size and population, are further subdivided into fifty provinces.

The thick forest surrounding this Catalonian town is characteristic of the Pyrenees Zone.

Spain's Cantabrian Zone, which lies along the northwest border of the country, includes the communities of Galicia, Asturias, Cantabria, La Rioja, and the Basque Country (País Vasco), known to Basque nationalists as *Askatasuna*. This wet northern region is dominated by the Cantabrian Mountains and lush, fertile hills and valleys. Swift streams tumble through the mountain ravines. A wide variety of crops are grown here, since winds blowing in from the Atlantic Ocean keep the area wet with rain. The region is also a center of Spain's fishing industry, which has been revitalized in recent years. The rugged coastline is dotted with small fishing towns (notable among which are Vigo and La Coruña), which keep the inhabitants supplied with lobster, shrimp, and crab. Because the mountains supply much of the country's coal and iron, the provinces of the Cantabrian Zone have become important industrial regions. Zinc, lead, and copper are also mined in large quantities.

To the east of the Cantabrian lies the Pyrenees Zone, extending from the Bay of Biscay to the Mediterranean Sea and consisting of Navarre (Navarra), Aragón, and Catalonia (Cataluña) (Spanish forms appear in parentheses). The Pyrenees mountain range stretches across this heavily forested part of Spain. Numerous streams course through the mountains, often forming glorious waterfalls as they plummet from the cliffs. The Ebro River also winds through the region, fed by tributaries that originate in the Pyrenees. Irrigation has helped transform the neighboring plains into productive farmland. Industry and tourism contribute to the wealth of the area, particularly in and around Catalonia's capital city, Barcelona, situated on the Mediterranean coast.

As one moves south from the provinces of "wet Spain," mountains give way to the wide expanse known as the Castilian tablelands, or *meseta*. This dry region—depicted in Miguel de Cervantes's classic novel, *Don Quixote*—encompasses almost half of mainland Spain and is divided into two main parts by the Central Sierra and Iberian mountains. The communities of Castile-León (Castilla y León), Extremadura, Castile-La Mancha (Castilla-La Mancha), and Madrid occupy this vast central plateau, with Madrid, the country's capital city, serving as the hub. Outside of Madrid, the countryside is sparsely populated, containing small towns separated by wide expanses of arid plains and occasional rolling hills and valleys. The continental climate of central Spain is characteristically hot in the summer and freezing cold in the winter. Grains such as wheat, rye, and corn are harvested

A network of rivers, such as this one in upper Aragón, makes productive farmland possible throughout northeastern Spain.

here, but much of the countryside is not irrigated and thus produces few crops. The barrenness of the region is exemplified by the Spanish proverb, "There is in Castile hardly a branch on which a bird may light."

The Andalusian Zone to the south consists of the eight provinces of Andalusia (Andalucía). The Spanish ranching industry is centered here; herds of cattle and flocks of sheep dotting the countryside are common sights. The Mediterranean climate of these lowlands is conducive to the cultivation of olives and grapes, the country's two most valuable commerical crops. Spain's only navigable river—the Guadalquivir (from the Arabic *Wadi el Kabir,* or "the Great River")—flows through this region. The lowlands adjacent to the river are the most fertile in all of Spain. Seville, a major port city, lies along the shores of the Guadalquivir, approximately sixty miles east of its mouth in the Gulf of Cádiz. Although not as prominent as in recent years, mining is still important to the region, with coal, copper, and lead among the major mineral resources.

The Mediterranean climate of Andalusia attracts tourists and enables the cultivation of grapes and olives.

Extending along the Mediterranean coastline is the narrow plain known as the Levant ("the East"). It runs from Valencia south through Murcia and ends in the easternmost part of Andalusia. Although much of the region is extremely arid, it is heavily irrigated and intensively cultivated. Rice, almonds, grapes, lemons, and the world-famous Valencia oranges are grown here in abundance. The warm climate and sandy beaches attract many tourists, who are the source of the largest percentage of the area's wealth. The town of Benidorm is one of the more popular resorts on the *Costa Blanca*, or "White Coast."

BEYOND THE MAINLAND

For centuries Spain was one of the world's great powers, ruler of a vast empire, but modern-day Spain's territorial possessions have shrunk to almost nothing. Two of its seventeen autonomous communities consist of island groups that remain under its control.

*The Canary Islands'
Pico de Teide, at 12,188
feet, is the highest point
in all of Spain.*

In the Mediterranean Sea, Spain governs the Baleares (Islas Baleares), an archipelago consisting of the islands of Majorca, Minorca, Ibiza, Cabrera, and Formentera, as well as eleven islets. Well known as resort areas, the islands are hilly and wooded. Fishing and farming are the main occupations, almonds, peaches, apricots, and tomatoes the main crops. Tourism, however, dominates the economy.

The Canary Islands (Islas Canarias), lying seventy miles off the northwestern coast of Africa, are volcanic in origin. The main islands of the group are Grand Canary, Fuerteventura, Lanzarote, Tenerife, La Palma, Gomera, and Hierro. The highest mountain peak in the chain—Pico de Teide, on Tenerife—is the highest point, at 12,188 feet, in all of Spain. The terrain at the base of the mountains, made fertile by the accumulation of volcanic ash, enables farmers to cultivate a variety of crops, with bananas and tomatoes prized around the world. Contrary to popular belief, the Canaries are not named for the small yellow bird, but rather for a breed of wild dog (*canes*) once prominent on the islands. As in the Baleares, tourism is important to the Canaries; Las Palmas and Santa Cruz de Tenerife are two favorite tourist destinations.

In addition to these possessions, Spain also administers two small enclaves in northern Africa. Along the Moroccan coast, the cities of Melilla and Ceuta, both military bases, gained limited autonomy in September 1994.

THE EARLIEST INHABITANTS

Although the land we know today as Spain first appeared in recorded history around the ninth century B.C., the Iberian Peninsula was home to a race of hunters as far back as Paleolithic times. Evidence of these people can be seen in the Altamira caves, near the city of Santander in Cantabria, on the northern coast. Anthropologists estimate the paintings of bison, elk, boar, and other animals that grace the walls and ceilings of the caves are nearly fifteen thousand years old.

Centuries later, beginning as early as 3000 B.C., inhabitants of northern Africa migrated north and fanned across the southern two-thirds of the Iberian Peninsula, reaching as far north as the Ebro River. The Iberian Peninsula derives its name from these early farmers, herdsmen, and miners ("dwellers along the Iberus," or Ebro River). These dark-skinned, clannish tribes lived in walled cities, isolated from one another and under no central authority. The most important of these city-states was Tartessos, whose mineral wealth was undoubtedly what attracted the Phoenicians, the first foreigners to arrive from the east. The Phoenicians settled along the Mediterranean coast around 1000 B.C. and founded the important trade center of Gades—the present-day city of Cádiz—at the southwestern tip of Spain. Cádiz is generally considered the oldest city in western Europe. The Phoenicians, skilled sailors, were responsible for opening the Mediterranean to commerce.

In time, Greek traders also arrived along the coast and introduced the cultivation of olives and grapes. The Phoenicians and Greeks occasionally journeyed through the Strait of Gibraltar, known at that time as the Pillars of Hercules for the two peaks which stood at opposite sides of this gateway to the Atlantic Ocean—exploring the western coast of Africa and venturing into parts of the Atlantic.

In the meantime, far to the north, another group of people had invaded the Iberian Peninsula. The Celts made their way south from what is now France in two separate waves, the first around 900 B.C. and the second approximately 250 years later. They traveled across the Pyrenees and settled in the northern part of Spain. Some of these farmers mixed with the native Iberian tribes in the northern and central regions to form the Celtiberians. Descendants of this fair-skinned group may be found today in the Cantabrian and Pyrenean Zones.

By the third century B.C., the powerful African state of Carthage, formerly a Phoenician colony, had shown interest in the Iberian area. Having been defeated by the Romans in the First Punic War, the Carthaginians advanced north to establish their authority in Spain. They conquered most of the coastal settlements, although the tribes of the interior were generally left alone. The great city of Barcelona was founded by the Carthaginians in 228 B.C.

Spain (Hispania) *thrived under Roman rule, eventually becoming the wealthiest region in the empire.*

This Carthaginian success in Spain was not viewed favorably by Rome, and new attacks on Roman territory by the Carthaginian general Hannibal eventually precipitated the Second Punic War. Again, the Romans were victorious and, by 205 B.C., the last Carthaginian city had been forced into submission, and Spain came under Roman jurisdiction.

ROMAN RULE

For the next two centuries, tribes in the central region continued to resist the Romans. Eventually, however, Spain became united as part of the great Roman Empire. For the next four hundred years, Spain developed rapidly under Roman rule. Hispania, as Spain was called by the Romans (possibly derived from the Carthaginian word *spania* meaning "land of the rabbits"), was initially divided into three provinces, soon thereafter increased to five—Tarraconensis, Carthaginensis,

THE SEGOVIA AQUEDUCT

The legacy of Roman rule in Spain is discernible in many areas, but nowhere more than in architecture, where Roman influence is apparent in the homes, theaters, bridges, and arenas of various regions. One of the best-preserved remaining engineering masterpieces of the Romans is the aqueduct of Segovia.

An aqueduct is a structure built for carrying water from its source to a remote destination. Modern aqueducts are systems that may be composed of pipelines, canals, and tunnels. Ancient ones were much more primitive. Known as *El Puente* ("The Bridge"), the Segovia structure was built by the Roman emperor Trajan (53–117) and is still in use. It transports water ten miles, from the Frío River to Segovia in the north-central community of Castile-León. It is constructed of more than twenty thousand dark-colored blocks of Guadarra-ma granite, fitted together without the use of either mortar or cement. The portion which runs above ground is nine hundred feet long and consists of 148 arches, each at least thirty feet high. Two levels of arches were required to support the center portion of the aqueduct due to a drop in the terrain. At that point, the structure stands more than ninety feet above the ground.

It is only fitting that this structure is one of the monuments that remains from Roman times, since the most extensive ancient system of aqueducts was that built by Rome. Segovia's eleven aqueducts totaled nearly three hundred miles in length and transported water as far as fifty-six miles.

The Segovia Aqueduct, built by the Romans almost two thousand years ago, is still used to transport water.

Baetica, Lusitania (mostly present-day Portugal), and Gallaecia. Each of these provinces was headed by a governor appointed by Rome.

The civilization of Roman Spain became unified as it had never been at any previous time in its history. This unification was made possible through the creation of common bonds of law, language, and communication. Romans and natives worked together to improve existing cities and towns and to build new ones. Roman engineers built roads to connect the cities, and aqueducts to bring water to the towns of the dry *meseta*. Latin became the official and generally accepted language of the country, although the Basques in the north retained their own tongue.

Although Roman culture was not imposed on the natives, much of it was assimilated. Wealthy Iberians were allowed to take an active role in the government. Eventually, all inhabitants were allowed to become citizens of the Roman Empire.

SAINT JAMES

According to legend, Saint James brought the gospel with him to the northern provinces of Spain in the middle of the first century in an effort to convert people to Christianity. Although there are no historic facts to support the legend, it has become an integral part of the religious tradition of the country.

Having met with little success, Saint James returned to Jerusalem, where he was beheaded by Herod Agrippa I, grandson of Herod the Great, in about A.D. 44. His followers placed his remains on a boat, which was miraculously transported to Spain, where he was buried.

His burial place, forgotten for eight hundred years, was miraculously discovered by Bishop Iria Flavia in Padrón, near the town of Compostela. King Alfonso II visited the site and ordered that an earthen church be built over the tomb. This was replaced some time later with a larger stone structure by Alfonso III.

James eventually became the patron saint of Spain under the name of Santiago (Sant Iago), and the shrine became one of the most important Christian pilgrimage sites in the entire world since medieval times. The authenticity of this sacred relic of Compostela, however, is still open to question.

As the economy expanded, Hispania soon became the wealthiest region in the entire empire. Olive oil, fruits, wine, and grains were produced in abundance, and iron, copper, and lead were mined in great quantities. Tons of gold and silver taken from local mines were exported to Rome. Hispania was also one of the empire's most cultured provinces. The writer Quintilian, the philosopher Seneca, and the poets Lucan and Martial were all born on the peninsula.

The most significant event under Roman rule was the introduction of Christianity to Hispania around the middle of the first century A.D., possibly by Saint Paul between the years 63 and 67. Christianity was embraced as the religion of the Roman Empire by Constantine in 312. By the fourth century, Hispania was predominantly Christian. Spain would adopt Catholicism as its official religion in 587. The church was establishing the strong foundation that would play a significant role in the nation's future.

THE VISIGOTHS

By the beginning of the fifth century, after four hundred years of relative peace and unity, the Roman Empire began to show signs of decline. After Theodosius I died in 395, the weakened Roman forces faced a new threat from the north. Invading Germanic tribes of Alans, Vandals, and Suevi swooped down across the Pyrenees and spread through the peninsula in 409. The Romans appealed to another Germanic tribe—the Visigoths—for help in ridding the land of the intruders. The Visigoths migrated into Spain from France and pushed the barbaric invaders south into present-day Andalusia (originally Vandalusia), and eventually they forced them into North Africa. The Visigoths then took control of most of Spain in the name of the Roman emperor and established Toledo as their capital. Soon, however, they broke their alliance with Rome.

The Visigoths, numbering less than 250,000, ruled over the 6 or 7 million inhabitants of the peninsula. They attempted to assimilate the Hispano-Roman culture and bring the separate populations together under their reign. More and more, however, the Visigoths themselves became romanized. Latin became the main language of the country, and many Visigoths converted to Catholicism during the reign of King Reccared.

A lack of unity led to the eventual fall of the Visigothic empire. Factions within the realm battled each other for control, and no central authority was recognized by all. Despite the problems and unrest that existed under Visigothic rule, it managed to last for nearly three hundred years. The final blow to Visigothic rule, however, came with the expanding hordes of Muslims in North Africa.

THE MOORS

The Muslims were Arabs who followed the teachings of Muhammad, the founder of a new religion called Islam, that had spread throughout much of the Middle East in the seventh century. These Muslims—called Moors by the Spanish because they were originally Moroccans—had shown interest in Hispania for many years. In 711, a contingent under the command of Tariq ibn Ziyad moved northward into the peninsula at a vast rock called Jabal Tariq (Arabic for "Mount Tariq"). This name was eventually corrupted to the current Gibraltar.

The Visigoths offered little resistance to the Moors after King Roderick, their general, was killed in battle. The Moors named the peninsula al-Andalus ("The Isle of the Vandals"), the area known to this day as Andalusia.

In addition to a new religion, the Moors brought with them a new Arabic language and culture. They shared their keen knowledge of the sciences with the natives and introduced new crops, such as oranges, pomegranates, figs, dates, and rice. Moor-

Moorish rule over Spain was marked by frequent warfare followed by long periods of peace.

ish architecture became prominent in the southern part of al-Andalus, as many ornate mosques (Islamic places of worship) and *alcázars* (palaces) were built. The Moors erected the city of Córdoba as their capital and made the cities of Seville and Granada into major centers of learning. Muslim scholars like Avicenna and Averroës made important contributions to Spanish culture.

Moorish rule was never centralized like that of Rome. Conflict was frequent and internal warfare punctuated long periods of peace. Even though Muslim rule was generally tolerant, many Christians converted to Islam because all religions did not enjoy equality under Muslim law.

Muslim rule prevailed in Spain for nearly three hundred years, and Arabic culture took hold and spread among many of the people. Moorish influence in the south of Spain can still be seen today, especially in the architecture of the Andalusian region. Under the Moors, Spain became known throughout Europe for its wealth and power.

The ornate detail seen in this fourteenth-century alcázar in Seville is characteristic of Moorish architecture.

All was not perfect, however. Fighting among local rulers continued. In addition, groups of Christians throughout the country—especially in the north—resented Moorish rule. Movements began among these groups to deter the Moors in their passage through the land and skirmishes between Christians and Moors resulted. The first of these engagements was organized by a Gothic noble named Pelayo, a king of Oviedo, who, in 722, defeated the Moors at Covadonga in Asturias. This marked the crude beginnings of what would eventually result in the *Reconquista,* or reconquest of Spain, nearly seven centuries later. By the early tenth century, the Christians had solidified their positions in the north in Asturias, Galicia, and León. As they recaptured land from the Moors, they built castles to guard their territory. The region thereafter became known as Castilla, or Castile ("Land of Castles").

The influence of the Moors is easy to see in the architecture of the Andalusian region.

When the Moors had first conquered Spain, the country was ruled by a representative of the Ummayad dynasty in the capital of Córdoba. Ummayad rule lasted until 1031, by which time Islamic Spain had been broken up into twenty *taifas,* or small kingdoms. The leaders of the *taifas* fought amongst themselves for control, and by 1085, only eleven remained. The resulting disorder inspired the Christians from northern Spain to advance the crusade of the Reconquest southward. The *taifa* kings panicked and looked for help from the Almoravids, Muslims who had conquered most of North Africa. The Almoravids were able to halt the Christian advance for a brief time. They then eliminated the *taifa* kings and reunited *al-Andalus* under one leader.

The Christians, however, did not give up the fight. The power of the Almoravids weakened, and by the middle of the twelfth century, Islamic Spain was once again a composite of *taifa* kingdoms. A new Islamic sect—the Almohads—came into power. By 1212, however, their hold had been broken. The fragmented Islamic kingdom would no longer prove to be a match for the Christian armies.

By the thirteenth century, despite occasional battles amongst themselves, the Christian kings had forced the Moors south to the region of the peninsula around Cádiz and the kingdom of Granada. The rest of Spain was divided between two major dominions: Castile and León in the west, and Aragón in the east.

An important event in the reunification of the peninsula occurred in 1469 when two royal cousins, Isabella of Castile and Ferdinand of Aragón, married. The royal couple soon made plans to complete the *Reconquista* and rid the country of the remaining Moors. In 1482, they began their offensive against Granada. Ten years later, Boabdil, ruler of Granada, surrendered, and the Moors were dislodged from their final stronghold. The effect of Muslim influence on Spanish civilization, however, would leave a much more indelible impression.

Religious Unification

After driving the Muslims from the peninsula, Ferdinand and Isabella—soon to become known as the "Catholic Monarchs"—attempted to unify their country's religious faith. A significant Islamic population remained, as well as a Jewish segment. (Some fifty thousand Jewish families had been transplanted to Hispania by the Roman emperor Hadrian.) The tool the monarchs used for carrying out this task was to become known as the Inquisition.

SPAIN (ca. 1450)

Originally, the Inquisition was instituted by Pope Sixtus IV in 1478, at the request of Ferdinand and Isabella, in order to identify and weed out those persons who had converted to Christianity without sincerely accepting the religion—*marranos* (converts from Judaism) and *moriscos* (converts from Islam). Over time, however, it became an instrument entirely controlled by the Spanish kings for persecuting all non-Christians. The Inquisition was presided over by a high council and grand inquisitor. The first of these inquisitors, Tomás de Torquemada, would become a symbol of brutality, intolerance, and religious zealousness. No one felt absolutely safe from the Inquisition. In time, even Saint Ignatius of Loyola and Saint Teresa of Ávila were investigated for possible heresy.

The Inquisition especially targeted Jews; many were banished from Spain.

Although the Spanish Inquisition is associated with cruelty and intolerance, in truth it was no more inhumane than similar institutions of the time in other countries, which likewise relied on torture, imprisonment, and execution. Sentences were carried out in public ceremonies known as autos-da-fé, or "acts of faith." By the time it was outlawed in 1834, the Inquisition had been responsible for an estimated three thousand to five thousand deaths.

One group particularly affected by the Inquisition was the Jews, who had been allowed to practice their faith by the Moors. Many Jews publicly converted to Catholicism, but continued to practice Judaism in private. By 1492 the Inquisition mandated the expulsion of all Jews who refused to be baptized as Catholics. (Soon after the beginning of the sixteenth century, a similar law was passed regarding Muslims.) Approximately 150,000 Jews were banished, with the majority relocating to Portugal, which had been recognized as a separate kingdom in 1143. Eventually, many Jews would migrate to Holland, having been expelled in turn from Portugal when Ferdinand and Isabella's daughter married the Portuguese king Emmanuel I.

During the Middle Ages, Spain had been a cultural intersection, with Christians, Muslims, and Jews living and working together—adding to the composite Spanish heritage. This spirit of cooperation (called *convivencia*) came to an end with the edicts of expulsion. In its stead, a religiously unified Spain was ready to extend its influence across the sea to the New World and to make its mark as a world power. This expansion and achievement would result because of the vision and efforts of a man named Christopher Columbus.

2

FINDING A PLACE
IN THE WORLD ORDER

No longer occupied with banishing the Moors, Spain began to turn its attentions outward. Shortly before the Moors were expelled from the country, an Italian named Christopher Columbus (Cristóbal Colón) came to Spain with a grand idea. Columbus dreamed of finding a new route to the Far East by sailing westward across the Atlantic Ocean, then known as the "Ocean Sea." He had tried unsuccessfully to interest the leading crowns of Europe in his dream. However, intrigued by visions of the riches and exotic goods to be gained, Isabella and Ferdinand agreed to sponsor Columbus's voyage in 1492.

Although he was unsuccessful in finding a new trade route to the Far East, Columbus did discover a whole new world. In the years that followed, other explorers traveled extensively while sailing under the Spanish flag. Vasco Núñez de Balboa became the first European to reach the Pacific Ocean in 1513. Hernán Cortés sailed to modern-day Mexico and conquered the Aztec empire (1519–1521). Ferdinand Magellan led an expedition on the first circumnavigation of the globe, after finding a passage around South America (1522). During this trip, Magellan also discovered and claimed the Philippines for Spain. Francisco Pizarro conquered the Incan civilization in Peru (1531–1533). Searching for gold in what would eventually become the southwestern United States, Francisco Vásquez de Coronado's soldiers became the first Europeans to sight the Grand Canyon and Colorado River (1540). Hernando de Soto led an expedition to what is now the southeastern United States, where he discovered the Mississippi River (1541).

Excited by the possibility of riches to be gained, Isabella and Ferdinand financed Columbus's search for a new route to the Far East.

Spurred by these initial successes, Spanish exploitation of the New World continued. As a result of the forays made by the early conquistadores, by 1550, Spain could lay claim to a large portion of the Americas. Gold and silver from Mexico and Peru poured into Castilian coffers, enriching the monarchy beyond its wildest dreams. Meanwhile, missionaries who traveled to these new lands brought the message of Christianity to the natives, constructed schools and churches, and taught the natives Spanish. Eventually Spanish became the official language in much of the New World, and it remains the most commonly spoken language in Latin America today.

EXPANDING SPAIN'S INFLUENCE IN EUROPE

With an eye toward expanding the Spanish sphere of influence in Europe as well as in the Americas, Ferdinand sought to solidify his country's interests on the continent. To do so, he created alliances with other realms through the marriages of his children. One daughter—Catherine of Aragón—married the heir to the English throne, while another—Isabella—married Prince Alfonso of Portugal. A third daughter—Juana—married into the German-Austrian Habsburg dynasty. This marriage bore Ferdinand a grandson, who became Charles I of Spain in 1516 upon Ferdinand's death. As a result of the marriage, Charles was also crowned Charles V of the Habsburgs of Germany and Austria and later named Holy Roman Emperor as Charles V. Unquestionably, Charles was the most influential Christian ruler of the time.

Having been raised outside of Spain, Charles was resented by many Spaniards as an outsider. In time, however, he won the loyalty of his subjects, in part due to his adherence to the ideals of his grandparents.

Charles's dream of solidifying his Catholic empire led him gradually into a series of conflicts with several European nations, including France, Germany, and Italy. Eventually, he found it impossible to accomplish his vision of a united Catholic Europe, as Protestantism took hold and gained momentum, particularly in Germany.

One problem faced by Charles in ruling an empire as wide ranging as Spain's was that it was difficult to maintain a centralized government. The empire consisted of many territories, each administered under its own rules and laws. This mirrored the situation found in Spain itself, where regions such as Castile, Aragón, and the Basque provinces were each subject to local laws. Upon his abdication in 1556, Charles decided to divide his holdings. His son Philip received control over his possessions in Spain, Italy, and the Netherlands,

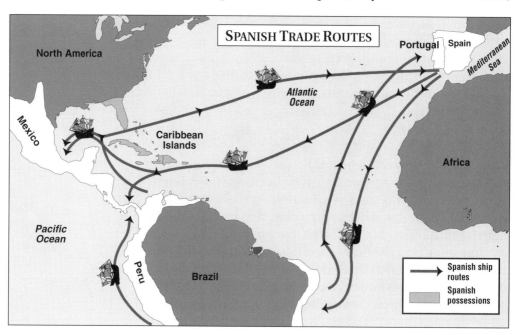

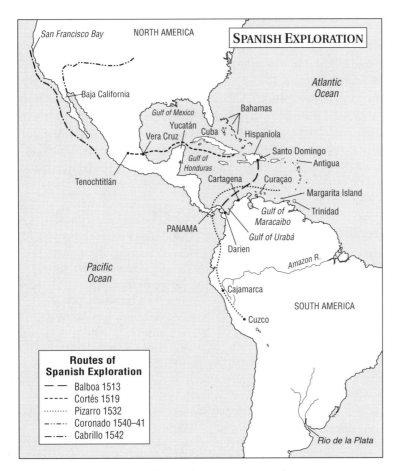

Routes of Spanish Exploration map showing SPANISH EXPLORATION with labels: San Francisco Bay, NORTH AMERICA, Baja California, Atlantic Ocean, Gulf of Mexico, Bahamas, Yucatán, Cuba, Hispaniola, Vera Cruz, Santo Domingo, Antigua, Gulf of Honduras, Cartagena, Curaçao, Tenochtitlán, Margarita Island, Gulf of Maracaibo, Trinidad, PANAMA, Gulf of Urabá, Darien, Amazon R., Pacific Ocean, Cajamarca, SOUTH AMERICA, Cuzco, Rio de la Plata.

Routes of Spanish Exploration

— — Balboa 1513
- - - - Cortés 1519
·········· Pizarro 1532
—··—·· Coronado 1540–41
—·—·— Cabrillo 1542

while his brother Ferdinand was given authority over Austria and the Holy Roman Empire.

Philip's reign was marked by even more warfare than that of his father. Spain waged battles against the Turks in the Mediterranean, against Protestant dissenters in the Netherlands, and against the English in response to attacks on Spanish ships by British pirates. The encounters with England proved to be disastrous. Philip believed that nothing short of total military victory would prevent England from helping the rebels in the Netherlands. In 1588, Philip launched the Spanish Armada, composed of 130 ships, to invade England. The fleet was demolished by a combination of raging storms and British forces. Only 67 of the ships made it back home to Spain. This demoralizing defeat marked a turning point in Spanish history. Spain was no longer powerful enough to impose its ideal of religious unity on Europe.

Spain's power continued to decline throughout the 1600s, economically, politically, socially, and militarily. Much of the wealth that had been acquired from the New World was used to finance the wars in Europe. This hampered the country's internal development. Various rulers imposed new taxes and borrowed money from foreign banks in an effort to stabilize the economy, but these proved to be only temporary solutions. Epidemics and famine further aggravated the situation, and Spanish kings were forced to declare bankruptcy

THE BLACK DEATH

Among the darkest episodes in Western history were the medieval outbreaks of plague that ravaged Europe. The pandemic, which raged through the middle and late fourteenth century, has become known as the Black Death.

Plague occurs in three forms in humans—bubonic, pneumonic, and septicemic. The bubonic variety is spread through the bites of insects who get the bacillus from rats, while pneumonic plague is spread through contact with infected persons. The Black Death was probably a combination of these two types. Symptoms of the plague include inflamed lymph nodes, headache, nausea, vomiting, high temperatures, and general fatigue. If untreated, death usually occurs within two or three days after the onset of symptoms. During the last few hours prior to death, the victim's skin takes on a purplish color due to respiratory failure. This dark skin tone led to the name Black Death.

Originating in Asia, the disease first spread to southern Europe in 1348 as a result of plague-infested corpses being catapulted by Kipchak (Turkic) warriors during an attack on a trading post in the Crimea. From there, it was transmitted throughout the Mediterranean region, eventually making its way northward through most of Europe and southward to North Africa. Reports vary, but most chronicles of the time suggest a mortality rate as high as two-thirds of the population in some regions. Rough estimates place the death toll in Europe at approximately 25 million. Aragón and Catalonia, in the northeastern part of the Iberian Peninsula, were especially hard hit.

The plague did not discriminate according to position or status. Among its victims were Eleanor, queen of Peter IV of Aragón, and King Alfonso XI of Castile.

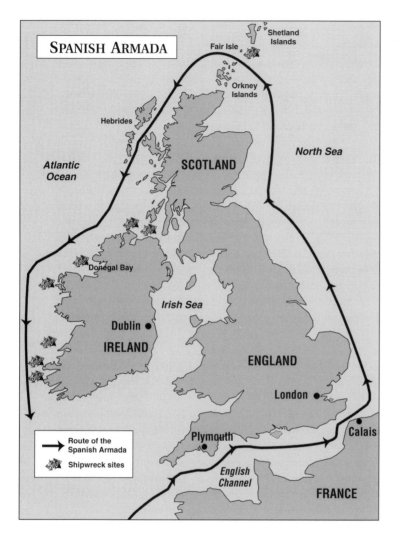

several times. The public turned more conservative and nationalistic, blaming all of their troubles on outsiders. Most
of the Moors remaining in Spain were expelled during this
period. This weakened the agricultural sector of the economy, since the great majority of Moors were hardworking
farmers.

Habsburg rule ended in Spain with the death of Charles II
in 1700. Charles willed the Spanish crown to his grand-
nephew, Philip of Anjou, who was a member of the French
Bourbon dynasty and a grandson of the French king Louis
XIV. Some European nations, however, were less than happy
with the idea of Bourbon power extending to Spanish

THE *ATOCHA*

Much of the riches and wealth that Spain extracted from the New World was used to finance the country's conflicts with England and France. Gold, silver, and other treasures were transported back to the homeland on cargo ships like the *Nuestra Señora de la Atocha.*

In April 1622, the *Atocha,* a 600-ton galleon, accompanied by a fleet of twenty-eight ships and commanded by Lope Díaz de Armendariz, the marquis of Cadereita, set sail for the Americas. By the time the boats reached Havana, Cuba, the *Atocha* was loaded with an immense treasure that included 901 silver bars, 161 gold bars, and more than a quarter of a million silver coins. The fleet planned to sail north up the east coast of Florida, then back to Spain. Unfortunately, due to unexpected delays, the ships did not sail until September 4, which was well into the hurricane season.

Within days, the seas became increasingly rough. Caught in a hurricane, the ships were separated and pushed off course. By the time the storms ended, eight ships had sunk—including the *Atocha*—and 550 people had gone to their final reward. The treasure on the *Atocha* would remain lost for over 350 years.

In 1970, American treasure hunter Mel Fisher began an extensive search for the *Atocha.* On July 20, 1985, sixteen years of searching finally paid off, and Fisher's team ultimately recovered almost forty-seven tons of silver, over 150,000 gold coins and bars, and millions of dollars in precious gems. This success did not come without a price, however, but at the expense of sixteen years of planning and searching, almost $10 million in equipment, and the lives of three divers, including one of Fisher's sons.

possessions, which led to the War of the Spanish Succession, from 1702 to 1714. The war found Spain, France, and Bavaria on one side, opposed by a Grand Alliance, which included the Austrian Habsburgs, Britain, the United Provinces of the Netherlands, and Portugal. Philip's coalition ultimately proved victorious, but in consequence, during the ensuing Peace of Utrecht, Spain lost many of its possessions in Italy, the Netherlands, and Gibraltar. As a result of this disastrous war, England emerged as the world's great naval, colonial, and commercial force. In addition, the war further strained relations among the provinces of Spain itself, and although Spain emerged from the fighting with its colonial empire intact, its political standing in Europe was greatly diminished.

In 1716, seeing that reform was a necessity, Philip V implemented changes in the Spanish system of government, transforming the country from a union of separate, autonomous regions into a more unified, centralized state. Reform continued through the century, as Spain endeavored to improve its economy. At the same time, Philip continued to strengthen his own authority while reducing the power of the Catholic Church and the nobility.

French influence in Spain was much in evidence during the reign of the Bourbon kings. Under the Bourbons, Spain generally sided with France in foreign matters and was antagonistic to Great Britain. In 1762, this resulted in Spain entering the Seven Years' War as a French ally. When Britain emerged victorious, Spain lost its claim in American Florida. However, it regained this interest in 1783 as one of the provisions of the Treaty of Versailles following yet another conflict with England. The last part of the century was marked by a relentless power struggle between Spain, France, and England.

LIBERALISM COMES TO SPAIN

When Napoléon Bonaparte came to power in France, French demands on Spain multiplied. In 1808, French armies invaded Spain. Napoléon forced the newly crowned king, Ferdinand, to abdicate and placed his brother Joseph on the Spanish throne. This interference in Spanish affairs on the part of France led to a widespread revolt among the Spanish citizenry. During the ensuing conflict, the term "guerrilla war," referring to an uprising of armed citizens rather than regular army soldiers, came into usage.

While this terribly ferocious war was raging, a new political consciousness began to take hold in the country. This was liberalism, based on the premise that political power should lie with the people, rather than with the monarch. A national assembly—the Cortes (Congress) of Cádiz—drafted a new constitution, which was proclaimed on March 19, 1812. The constitution took power from the king and placed it in the hands of the people in a Cortes elected by all Spanish males age twenty-five or above. Thus, the entire structure of Spanish society changed, as the powers of the aristocracy and clergy were diminished.

The Constitution of Cádiz was short-lived, however. When the combined armies of Spain, Portugal, and Britain forced France out of Spain to end the Peninsular War (called the War of Independence in Spain), Bourbon rule returned. When he was restored to the throne, Ferdinand VII revoked the new constitution. Although Ferdinand had returned power to the monarchy, liberalism continued to gain followers, especially in the army and among the middle and lower classes. The constitution was briefly restored during a revolution led by army officers in 1820, but Spain remained politically divided between the progressive and conservative liberals.

The weak and divided government faced many internal problems. Several of Spain's colonies in the Americas used this as an opportunity to break free from Spanish rule. By 1825, Cuba and Puerto Rico were the only New World colonies still under the Spanish flag. The once-great Spanish empire had been reduced even further.

After the defeat of Napoléon in 1814, King Ferdinand enters Madrid to reclaim his throne.

It was not until Ferdinand died in 1833 that the idea of a constitutional government became firmly entrenched. First, however, a struggle for power arose between Ferdinand's brother, Carlos, and supporters of his infant daughter, Isabella, the named heir to the throne. The result was the outbreak of a six-year civil war between Carlos's advocates—called "Carlists"—and Isabella's—called "Cristinos," after Isabella's mother who acted in her behalf. The Carlists were defeated, but bitterness remained. Tension between the two sides produced a series of conflicts that dragged on until Isabella eventually fled Spain in 1868.

A new solution to end the internal problems of the country was tried in 1873 when the First Republic was established. This was the earliest attempt in Spain at a republican government (one managed by elected representatives). Each of the country's provinces governed itself, which led to weakened central power in Madrid. The experiment ended in failure after a year's time, and once again Bourbon rule returned to Spain when Isabella's son, Alfonso XII, assumed the throne.

CONFLICTS OVERSEAS

Spain's problems overseas continued as well. Many Cubans had been clamoring for independence since 1868, when the Ten Years' War erupted. Peace was eventually reached in 1878, but only after two hundred thousand lives had been lost. The Treaty of El Zanjón, which marked the end of the war, stipulated that slavery be abolished in Cuba and governmental reforms be introduced. It was the failure of Spain to honor some of the terms of this treaty that set the stage for the Spanish-American War.

U.S. troops enter Ponce, Puerto Rico, after Spain's forced surrender of the island.

In 1898, the battleship *USS Maine* was sent to Cuba to protect American citizens living there. When the ship was destroyed and 260 lives lost in a mysterious explosion in Havana harbor on February 15, the media blamed Spain. The United States declared war on Spain two months later. Within months, Spain suffered a humiliating defeat when its navy was overwhelmed by U.S. forces at Santiago de Cuba and in Manila Bay. In Cuba, ground forces, including the famous Rough Riders of Teddy Roosevelt, were victorious at the Battles of El Caney and

San Juan Hill. Under the terms of the Treaty of Paris, which ended the war, Spain was forced to surrender Puerto Rico, Guam, and the Philippine Islands to the United States. The treaty also granted Cuba its independence, and the once-great Spanish empire was all but dissolved. An additional consequence of the Spanish-American War was the ascension of the United States to world power status.

CHANGES ON THE HORIZON

As Spain entered the twentieth century, it appeared obvious that changes had to be made. A group of writers and intellectuals known as the "Generation of 1898" forced Spaniards to look at themselves honestly and to face the reality that Spain was no longer a world power. Farm laborers, industrial workers, and army officers raised their voices to express displeasure with their situations. Discontented Spaniards began to organize unions in an attempt to voice their causes. The National Confederation of Labor (*Confederación Nacional del Trabajo*—CNT), founded in 1911, held a dominant position in the workers' movement until the eruption of the Spanish Civil War in 1936. Many new political parties formed, and the Spanish Socialist Workers' Party (*Partido Socialista Obrero Español*—PSOE) grew impressively. Regional sentiment in Catalonia, Galicia, and the Basque provinces further threatened the unity of the country, as the government demonstrated its inability to deal with its problems.

During World War I, Spain remained neutral, but the effects of the war caused turmoil in the nation's economy. While the industrialized regions of the north turned out products in record quantities, and farms and mines increased production, workers clamored for higher wages and better working conditions. Motivated by news of the Russian Revolution, socialists and anarchists led a general strike in 1917. It was quickly put down by the army, but hundreds of lives were lost during the subsequent years as violence between various sectors of the community became common.

During this period, Spain was engaged in an expensive, ongoing conflict in Morocco (1909–1926). A disastrous battle at Annual in 1921 saw fourteen thousand troops slaughtered by Moorish tribesmen. The weakened Spanish army could do little to help restore law and order in the homeland while engaged in this unpopular and difficult war.

As turmoil and discontent in Spain increased, faith in the constitutional monarchy and its current king, Alfonso XIII, waned. Thus, when in 1923 General Miguel Primo de Rivera led a military revolt to take over the government, Alfonso accepted the coup and made Primo de Rivera the head of the government. Although Spain enjoyed a brief period of economic and social improvement, the new military dictator was unable to accomplish all that he hoped to and he relinquished power in 1930.

As ever, dissatisfaction with the monarchy caused citizens to vote overwhelmingly for a republican form of government in the 1931 elections. Convinced that the country was on the brink of civil war, Alfonso vacated the throne. The Second Republic's new democratic constitution was adopted by the Spanish parliament, known as the Cortes. Under the new constitution, which stipulated the separation of church and state, the Catholic Church was forced to surrender much of its power and influence. Other constitutional provisions guaranteed equality before the law, bestowed the right to vote on all men and women over the age of twenty-three, abolished titles for nobility, and established free and compulsory education by the government.

The church and large landowners feared their loss of power. Also, a worldwide depression created a lack of confidence in the new government, and the result was widespread dissatisfaction, often expressed in the form of violence. The number of strikes increased, and the frustration felt by the Spanish people produced confrontation upon confrontation. The 1933 elections saw power returned to radical right-wing elements, which set out immediately to undo the previous government's reforms. Efforts to bring order to the land failed, however, and socialist revolts broke out in Catalonia and Asturias. Both sides suffered heavy casualties before the army was able to put down the insurrections. When the ruling coalition fell in 1935, civil war appeared imminent.

THE SPANISH CIVIL WAR

In early 1936, the Popular Front—a new leftist coalition party supported by the working classes—came into power, winning an electoral majority in the February elections. Political conservatives, however, feared the country was headed toward socialism, with the state taking over ownership of farms, industries, and banks. These conservatives, backed by

General Francisco Franco, shown here in 1936, led the Nationalists during the Spanish Civil War.

the military, launched an offensive against the leftists in July. Led by General Francisco Franco, who had forged his reputation during the Moroccan wars for independence from Spain, the rebels—known as Nationalists—captured several towns in southern Spain and began moving north. When they attempted to take Madrid, government forces—called Loyalists— fought back, and in time, many other forces joined the fray. American and European sympathizers, mainly intellectuals, writers, artists, and those politically committed to the leftist cause, fought on the side of the Loyalists, who also received military aid from the Soviet Union. The other side, the Nationalists, received support from both fascist Italy and Germany.

After nearly three years of violence and bloodshed, Franco's forces controlled much of the western part of the country. Barcelona fell to the Nationalists in January 1939, and Valencia, the temporary capital, fell in March. When Madrid surrendered later that month, the matter was decided, and Victory Day was celebrated by the Nationalists on the first day of April.

The Spanish Civil War decimated Spain. More than six hundred thousand Spaniards lost their lives in the fighting, and thousands more were injured. Additional thousands would die in the coming years, as Franco set about using military rule to purge the nation of his enemies by executing or imprisoning Loyalist supporters by the score. The countryside lay in ruins, and Franco found himself faced with the monumental task of trying to rebuild the nation.

THE FRANCO YEARS

Franco declared himself *caudillo,* or military leader, of the country. His dictatorship was supported by both the military and the Catholic Church. In 1937, Franco declared the Falange, the Spanish Fascist Party founded in 1933 by José

Antonio Primo de Rivera, son of the former dictator, to be the official party of the state and the only legal political party in Spain.

The rebuilding of Spain progressed slowly. The country faced extreme economic adversity, since much of the legislation favoring workers had been revoked. The first decade of Franco's rule, known as "the hungry years," was a time of scarcity and deprivation. Even food rationing failed to provide everyone with the basic necessities of life. Low agricultural output, in turn, retarded the nation's industrial development, and factory production fell to prewar levels.

Because of the country's ties to Italy and Germany, democratic nations of the world cut off all economic affiliations with Spain. Throughout the war, Franco retained ties with the Axis powers by sending them raw materials, as well as troops to support the German invasion of Russia. After World War II, despite its neutrality claim, Spain was barred from membership in the newly formed United Nations, since Franco was viewed as the "last of the fascist dictators."

Spain continued to suffer economically after the war as the United States and the Allies boycotted trade. It was not until the Cold War made enemies of the United States and the Soviet Union that the boycott was lifted. Official censure of Franco eased because of his stance against communism. In 1953, the United States took advantage of Spain's strategic position in Europe. The two countries signed the Pact of Madrid by which the United States agreed to give financial and economic aid to Spain in return for the right to establish four military bases on Spanish soil. Franco continued to modify his profascist stance, and Spain was finally granted membership in the United Nations in 1955.

Change did not come easily under Franco's rule, but it came nonetheless. The Stabilization Plan of 1959 laid the foundation for Spain's remarkable economic reversal. It instituted measures aimed at keeping inflation in check while, at the same time, encouraging foreign investment and trade. Within two years foreign capital investment grew sevenfold. Agricultural and industrial production began to increase. More people moved to the cities, as government-sponsored programs were instituted. By 1961, rapid industrial growth and an upsurge in tourism signaled an economic boom. Spain's standard of living began to show a dramatic increase.

THE ABRAHAM LINCOLN BRIGADE

Shortly after the Spanish Civil War began in 1936, some twenty-eight hundred Americans—the majority of whom were idealistic students—volunteered to fight side by side with the communists and Loyalist forces of the Spanish Republic in the battle against General Francisco Franco's pro-fascist troops. These courageous Americans became known as the Abraham Lincoln Brigade. Together with approximately thirty-five thousand other volunteers from various countries, they formed the International Brigades.

These undisciplined fighters, lacking military experience, stood little chance against Franco's troops, who received support from both Germany and Italy in the form of planes, weapons, and other supplies. Approximately nine hundred Americans lost their lives on Spanish soil. When the International Brigades were disbanded in November 1938, they were honored with a military parade in Barcelona. In a farewell speech, Spanish parliament member Dolores Ibarruri ("La pasionara") thanked the volunteers, telling them, "You may go proud. We shall not forget you."

The U.S. government, however, did not feel the same way. The volunteers had gone to Spain against the government's wishes, partly due to the country's fear of arousing Hitler's anger. Most of the volunteers were either communists, or they had been recruited by Comintern, the international communist movement. Upon their return home, they were put under surveillance by the Federal Bureau of Investigation.

In 1996, Spain marked the sixtieth anniversary of its civil war. More than 350 former members of the International Brigades returned for the observances. "We fought to defend democracy and defeat fascism," recounted Brooklyn-born Milton Wolff, the last commander of the Abraham Lincoln Brigade. To honor these men and women, the Cortes voted to grant Spanish citizenship to any who requested it.

Several thousand Americans fought against General Franco's troops in the Spanish Civil War.

By the 1970s, Spain enjoyed the fastest growing economy in all of Europe.

Strengthening of the economy led to a better-educated working class and an increased number of university students. Increasingly, Franco's restrictive policies were questioned, and increased tensions led to social unrest, strikes, and bombings. A series of liberal fundamental laws enacted in the late 1960s eased some legal restrictions and gave the country hope for additional individual liberties in the future. One of these laws allowed for greater freedom of the press; another refined the powers of the Cortes.

The growing tide of regional nationalism in Catalonia and the Basque Country became a growing problem. A new Basque separatist group, *Euskadi ta Askatasuna* ("Basque Homeland and Freedom," the ETA) launched terrorist attacks against the military. Luis Carrero Blanco, Franco's first prime minister and handpicked successor as the head of the government, was one of the victims of the ETA. His assassination in December 1973 was the group's most daring act of defiance. The government responded with reprisals of its own in an attempt to suppress the dissidents.

The problems facing Spain took more and more of a toll on the *caudillo*, as did medical problems. Finally, on November 20, 1975, Francisco Franco Bahamonde died, after having ruled Spain with an iron hand for thirty-six years.

JUAN CARLOS I

In 1947, Franco proclaimed the Law of Succession. Under this ruling, his successor would have the title of king. Since royal family members had supported the Nationalists during the Civil War, Franco felt that rule by a monarchy best suited Spain. He picked Juan Carlos de Borbón, the grandson of the last king, Alfonso XIII, to succeed him. Franco, the boy's self-appointed guardian, oversaw the prince's education, preparing him for his future position.

Upon Franco's death, however, rather than continuing his predecessor's authoritarian rule, Juan Carlos eased restrictions and began to overturn the framework erected by Franco. Greater freedom of the press was granted and public demonstrations were permitted. A new prime minister, Adolfo Suárez González, was appointed by Juan Carlos in

Juan Carlos I rejected his predecessor's authoritarian rule. Instead, he established a parliamentary democracy.

1976. Together, the two men were able to bring about a peaceful transition to democracy. The Law of Political Reform was passed, reestablishing Spain as a democratic nation with a bicameral legislature. The following June, Spain held its first free elections in forty years, with the Union of the Democratic Center (*Unión de Centro Democrático*— UCD) winning the greatest share of the vote.

The next year, a new democratic constitution was approved by parliament and by national referendum. It formally established a parliamentary democracy, with Juan Carlos as head of state, and created a legislature consisting of the Congress of Deputies and the Senate. Among the constitution's provisions was Article 2, which "recognizes and guarantees the right to autonomy of the nationalities and regions of which it is composed and the common links that bind them together." This set the stage for the formation of Spain's seventeen "autonomous communities" by 1983, with home rule privileges extended to each. Such considerations were not enough for Basque separatists, however, and terrorist activities increased.

Juan Carlos's effectiveness as a leader was demonstrated in February 1981 when rebel soldiers led by Colonel Antonio Tejero Molina invaded the Spanish parliament in an attempted military coup. While millions watched on television, Juan Carlos was able to defuse the situation, firmly maintaining that law and order would triumph. "The crown," he would later state, "symbol of the permanence and unity of the nation, cannot tolerate, in any form, actions or attitudes attempting to interrupt the democratic process."[2]

MODERN SPAIN

The Socialist Party came into power with the 1982 elections, and Felipe González Márquez became the new prime minister. At first, socialist programs sparked an economic recovery, stimulated by Spain's entry into the European Economic Community (now known as the European Union). Membership in the EEC and in the North Atlantic Treaty Organization (NATO), which Spain joined in 1982, gave the country a more influential role in European and world affairs.

In time, however, it became obvious that problems still remained. Spain's unemployment rate soared to nearly 25 percent—the highest of any Western European nation—and the peseta (Spain's monetary unit) was devalued several times. In addition, the ETA was continuing to use terrorist tactics to try to further their agenda of securing an independent Basque homeland.

The Popular Party made a strong showing in the 1993 elections, but the Socialists maintained their hold, despite falling short of an overall parliamentary majority. On January 27, 1994, much of the country was shut down by a general strike to protest a loosening of labor laws. These laws made it easier to fire and transfer workers. The government was further plagued by sensational accusations of corruption and scandal, and it soon became apparent that socialist rule was near an end.

In 1996, the conservative Popular Party emerged victorious, winning a plurality in the general elections. José María Aznar López was appointed prime minister as the head of a coalition government, bringing an end to sixteen years of socialist rule. As Spain prepared to enter the twenty-first century, much work remained to be done.

3

A Spectrum of Ethnic Communities

With nearly 40 million inhabitants, Spain is Europe's fifth most populous nation. Several of its regions have unique cultural, ethnic, and linguistic flavors. Food, holidays, even language vary from one part of the nation to another. Since the restoration of democracy in 1975, the heritage of each region has been allowed to emerge more than in years past. No longer are local traditions prohibited as they were during Franco's regime.

Each of these cultures adds its own individuality to the mixture which is Spain. The hardiness of the Castilians, the independence of the Basques, the romanticism of the Andalusians, and the spirit of the Gypsies can all be found in the Spanish personality.

Ethnic Variety

Most Castilians, who occupy the arid central region of Spain, reside in widely separated towns and villages. Having lived in this relative isolation for hundreds of years, Castilians are conservative and not as quick to accept change as the inhabitants of other regions. Even small farmers live in clusters of homes, as they have since the time when it was a necessity in order to protect themselves from invading armies. Like the land they till, Castilians are a hardy breed, robust and tireless. Three out of every four Spaniards speak Castilian Spanish, or *castellano*, which has been the official language of the country since 1230, due to the dominance of the once-powerful kingdom of Castile.

Approximately 16 percent of the population of Spain is Catalan, most of whom live in the four provinces of Catalonia in the northeast corner of the peninsula. There are other

Catalan communities in Valencia, Aragón, and the Balearic Islands. Outside of Spain, Catalans may be found in Andorra and in southern France. The majority of Catalans live in Barcelona province, one of the most highly populated and richest areas of Spain. The region is highly industrialized, and many migrant workers relocate here from other parts of the country. These hard-working migrants learn to speak Catalan, which has similarities to Italian and Provençal as well as to Spanish. Catalans are industrious and business-minded and more open to strangers than their Basque neighbors to the west.

The Basques, known for their love of freedom and independence, speak Euskera, *the only known representative of its own language family.*

Living in the rugged northwestern corner of Spain, Galicians have an intense attachment to their homeland. The region has remained agrarian and is relatively poor. Farmland is subdivided into tiny plots known as *minifundios.* These holdings are so small that most of the natives can earn no more than a subsistence-level income. This has caused many Galicians to migrate to other, more productive regions. Galician, or *Gallego,* the official language of this "wet Spain" zone, is also spoken in parts of Portugal.

The 3 million or so Basques living in Spain are centered in the communities of the Basque Country and Navarre, along both sides of the Pyrenees on Spain's northern border. The Basques are a fiercely proud people, freedom loving and independent. Among the oldest groups in all of Europe, they, more than any other group, have resisted identifying with Spain as a whole, preferring instead to maintain their traditional culture and values. These traditions, however, have been in decline since the introduction of heavy industry to the region; but a core of separatists still clamor for independence from Spain. *Euskera,* the language spoken by Basque natives and the most distinctive of the languages spoken in Spain, has been in decline for centuries. It is generally passed on as an oral language rather than a written one. Usage by

Still living much as they did centuries ago, Gypsies can still be found all over the world. Here, a Spanish Gypsy, or gitana, *performs a traditional dance.*

individual families, as opposed to formal instruction in schools, has kept the language alive.

The name Gypsies refers to a group of people who are believed to have migrated to Europe from the Hindu Kush region of northern India as early as the eleventh century. Members refer to themselves as Rom and speak a language called *Romani,* which is related to Sanskrit. In Spain, however, Romani has blended with Spanish to form the hybrid language known as *Lengua Caló.* An estimated two hundred thousand Gypsies call Spain their home. This is a very rough estimate, however, because many still lead a nomadic existence and a census is difficult. The largest group—the *gitanos*—have settled in the cities of Andalusia in southern Spain. Many still make their living as coppersmiths, horse dealers, singers, dancers, and fortunetellers. Discrimination against Gypsies, widespread for centuries, continues to the present day. Modern Gypsies, however, have created organizations such as the Union of the Gypsy People to combat such prejudice.

Although they do not have their own language, Andalusians are also considered a culturally distinct community. Living in the eight southernmost provinces of the country, many are descendants of the Moors who populated the region prior to the Reconquest. Like their predecessors, the people of Andalusia are often more sensuous and emotional than the inhabitants of other regions. Economically, the region is one of the poorest in the country. Unlike in Galicia, the land in Andalusia was divided into large *latifundios* following the Reconquest. These large estates were owned by a small percentage of the population and worked by day laborers who wandered the countryside in search of jobs. This

economic system was not very productive, and many Andalusians migrated to other regions of the country.

Madrid, the Hub of Spain

Lying on the banks of the Manzanares River in the geographical center of the country, Madrid is the capital of
Spain, as well as its largest city, with a population of just over
3 million. Located on the *meseta,* it is the political, financial,
and transportation center of the country. Madrid is an important manufacturing center, and its factories produce mo-
tor vehicles, aircraft, processed food, leather goods, and
chemicals.

Opus Dei

In 1928, José María Escrivá de Balaguer y Albas,
a lawyer in Aragón who had become a priest, founded a group
that would eventually be recognized as the first secular religious institution of the Roman Catholic Church. The Prelature
of the Holy Cross and Opus Dei, or simply Opus Dei ("Work of
God"), is an international body with nearly eighty thousand
members worldwide. Its stated mission is to "remind all Christians that in whatever secular activity they dedicate themselves to they must cooperate in solving the problems of
society in a Christian way, and bear constant witness to their
faith." Members promise to use their professional skills in
God's service and to try to gain converts through their actions
and practices.

The group's activities in Spain came to the attention of the
government during the period of Franco's rule. Although Opus
Dei denied any political goals, its constituency began to as-
sume crucial roles in the government. Members occupied key
positions, including several posts in the cabinet. Influential
business leaders and university professors were members of
Opus Dei. They were responsible, in part, for introducing and
administering the programs that helped stabilize Spain's
economy. Because of the aura of secrecy surrounding the organization, in some circles it became known as the "Holy
Mafia." Much of Opus Dei's influence was lost following the
death of Prime Minister Luis Carrero Blanco, rumored to be an
Opus Dei member, in a spectacular explosion in Madrid in
1973.

Madrid's location in the geographic center of the country has led to its becoming the political, financial, and transportation center of Spain.

Madrid first emerged in history as the tenth-century Moorish fortress of Magerit, or Majrít. Philip II moved his court to the city in 1561, but it was not until 1607, under Philip III, that Madrid officially became the capital of Spain. It grew slowly but steadily, eventually becoming a sprawling metropolis.

Although it boasts many tall, modern buildings, Madrid also retains much of its Old World charm. *Madrileños* still close down their businesses to take a three-hour siesta at midday when the temperature is at its zenith. People wander the broad, tree-lined avenues, exploring the outdoor squares and myriad shops and enjoying the beautiful parks and gardens. The city is home to the renowned Prado Museum of Art, the Reina Sofia Art Center, the Spanish Museum of Contemporary Art, and the Joaquín Sorolla Museum. The Royal Palace, traditional home of Spanish kings, is another tourist attraction in the city honored by the European Union in 1992 as the "Cultural Capital of Europe." The world's largest bullring—Plaza de Toros Monumental de las Ventas—is also located in Madrid.

BARCELONA

The magnificent port city of Barcelona was founded as Barcino in 230 by the Carthaginian general Hamilcar Barca (father of Hannibal). It lies on the country's Mediterranean coastline, surrounded by mountains. Barcelona is Spain's second-largest city (population 1.6 million) and the capital of the community of Catalonia. The busiest industrial city in Spain, Barcelona produces textiles, machinery, chemicals, and paper.

Through the years, Barcelona has been the center of Catalan regionalism. It was a Loyalist stronghold during the Spanish Civil War until captured by the Nationalists in 1939. Heavy industry and tourism have helped the city build a reputation as the most prosperous metropolis in Spain. Massive municipal programs, stimulated by Barcelona's selection as the site of the 1992 Summer Olympics, helped spur the city's development.

An enormous statue of Christopher Columbus marks the entrance to the Rambla, the thoroughfare that leads from the harbor to the heart of the city. Tiny squares, fountains, and cafés mark the narrow, cobbled streets, while the skyline is punctuated by buildings both modern and historic. La Sagrada Familia cathedral, in a newer section of Barcelona, is one of Spain's most famous landmarks. The Picasso Museum and the Museum of Art of Catalonia also attract many tourists, as does the Museo d'Història de la Ciutat (City History Museum), which features an underground tour through excavated sections of old Barcelona.

OTHER MAJOR CITIES

Valencia, the third-largest city in Spain (population 750,000), lies at the mouth of the Tura River on the Mediterranean coastline, some 220 miles south of Barcelona. The city is an agricultural center, developed through widespread irrigation. Oranges, lemons, almonds, and dates, exported by way of the excellent harbor, have made Valencia one of Spain's most prosperous cities. Tourism is another strong source of income for the Valencia region. Thousands flock to the beautiful beaches of the Costa Blanca (White Coast). Others come annually in March to take part in the *fallas de Valencia,* or Fire Festival. During this weeklong feast of Saint Joseph, huge sculptures depicting famous people or events in Spanish history are erected at intersections around the city. At midnight on the final night, the figures are set afire and fireworks light up the sky. This event has been cited by some as one of the greatest spectacles in all of Europe. Cultural attractions in Valencia include the Palacio de Marqués de Dos Aguas, the Museo de Bellas Artes, and the Institute of Modern Art.

Seville (population 660,000) is the capital of Andalusia. It reached the height of its glory during the voyages of discovery to the Americas. Due to its location on the banks of the Guadalquivir River and its accessibility to oceangoing vessels, Seville became the center of Atlantic trade, and wine, olives, and oranges were shipped west in major quantities. Earlier, under the Moors, Seville (originally called Hispalis in ancient times) had been an important cultural center. Moorish architecture can still be found throughout the city, the most prominent example being the Alcázar, a palace that dates back to 1181. Another popular site for tourists is the magnificent Gothic cathedral, which stands on the spot once occupied by a twelfth-century mosque. The cathedral is the third-largest church in the world, after Saint Peter's in Rome and Saint Paul's in London. More recently, Seville was the site of Expo '92, which marked the five-hundredth anniversary of the discovery of the New World by Columbus.

Despite the many squares, churches, monasteries, and convents built after Ferdinand and Isabella reclaimed Granada from the Moors in 1492, the city is known for its Moorish architecture.

The city of Córdoba (population 300,000), on the Guadalquivir River, stands today as a reminder of the once-great Moorish empire. In its time, it was considered the largest, wealthiest, and most civilized city in all of Europe. An important metropolis as early as Phoenician times, this center of trade and learning was known as "the jewel of the world."[3] Córdoba is the site of the Great Mosque, which was constructed in the eighth century. Converted into a Christ-

ian church in 1236, it covers six acres and consists of some 850 pillars, linked together by horseshoe arches, which support the structure. It is the most glorious example of Moorish architecture ever constructed.

The Andalusian city of Granada was built on the site of a Roman settlement called Illiberis. It was the final stronghold of Moorish civilization on the Iberian Peninsula from the 1200s until 1492, when it was reclaimed for Spain by King Ferdinand and Queen Isabella. The most famous attraction in Granada is the ornate Moorish palace and fortress called the Alhambra. It was constructed between 1238 and 1358, during the reigns of Ibn al-Ahmar and his successor, and built of reddish brick called *tapia*, which gave it its name (*al hambra* means "the red one" in Arabic). The only medieval Arabic palace in the world that still survives intact, the Alhambra was called "one of the most remarkable, romantic and delicious spots in the world"[4] by writer Washington Irving. Ferdinand and Isabella were so taken with this beautiful structure that they made it their own residence when Granada was seized to complete the Reconquest. Today, their final resting place is in a double tomb in the Royal Chapel next to the cathedral.

The intricate filigree walls that surround the Court of the Lions help make the Alhambra the most beautiful surviving example of Western Islamic architecture.

The city of Toledo (population 64,000) lies just south of Madrid in central Spain on the banks of the Tagus River. Toledo, a former capital of Spain, contains an intermingling of every culture that ever invaded the province. Breathtaking religious edifices of Jews, Muslims, and Christians alike can be seen in this city, which was known as Toletum to the Romans. A landmark for travelers is the Cathedral of Toledo, with its 295-foot-high tower, beautiful murals, stained-glass windows, and works of El Greco, Velázquez, and Goya. The El Greco Museum is a major attraction for art aficionados. This ancient city of narrow winding streets is a national monument and center of learning and the arts.

FAMILY AND HOME LIFE

Everyday life in modern Spain is not much different from that in other Western European nations. However, as more and more people have moved from rural areas to the cities, the pace of living has picked up appreciably. This has brought about changes in the quality of daily life though, arguably, not necessarily for the better. People rush to and from jobs, eat meals at fast-food restaurants, and pollute the air with emissions from speeding cars.

A larger portion of the school-age population today continues its education in secondary schools and universities in the hope of obtaining better-paying jobs. Many more women have entered the workplace, creating higher average family income to spend on goods and services. Young people, especially, take advantage of increased prosperity to keep up with the latest trends in fashion, music, and other forms of entertainment. These distractions, in turn, have resulted in a diminished role for the church in most people's lives.

However, life in the country continues at a slower pace. Farmers persist in their struggle to earn a decent living to enable them to support their families. The luxuries of life are not a priority when the necessities have not been satisfied. Donkey carts and wagons can still be found making their way along country roads. Video games, computers, and CD players are far less likely to be seen in the country than in the cities. In such an environment, where consumerism has not intruded to a great degree, it is not surprising that the church is still often the center of village life.

FOOD

Like the multiplicity of people who constitute the country, Spanish food is a blend of many ingredients. Although it varies from region to region, its preparation is rather simple and the basic ingredients predominate. An exception is the cooking of Catalonia and the Basque provinces, where the cuisine is much more elaborate. Many consider Basque-style cooking the best in Spain.

Spanish cooking is usually thought to be very spicy, but that is a misconception. Pork is the most widely eaten meat, but lamb is often consumed on special occasions. The national dish is *cocido,* a heavy stew consisting of boiled meats, chicken, and vegetables. The best-known dish, however, is

paella. This dish, which originated in Valencia, is a colorful combination of meats, seafood, vegetables, and rice. Other popular native treats include gazpacho (a cold vegetable soup), empanadas (small meat pies), chorizo (sausage), and *arroz con pollo* (chicken with rice). Seafood is a diet staple in a country with such a considerable coastline.

Paella, a saffron-flavored medley of meats, seafood, vegetables, and rice, is Spain's most popular dish.

Spaniards generally drink beer and wine with meals, although bottled waters and soft drinks are available. Coffee is the almost universal drink after meals and at breakfast. *Sangría* is a popular summer drink made with red wine, various fruits, sugar, soda water, and a dash of liqueur. Rioja and sherry are two well-known Spanish wines produced in abundance.

Most Spaniards begin their day with a light breakfast. Lunch, generally served between two and three o'clock in the afternoon, is usually the main meal of the day, an ample repast consisting of multiple courses. Thus, supper is generally a lighter meal and is not eaten until nine o'clock at night or later.

TAPAS

Because the evening meal in Spain is usually not eaten before 9 P.M., Spaniards have developed a refined taste for snacks between meals. Catering to this passion, tapas bars have become extremely popular in Spain.

Tapas are small portions of food served with a drink. The word tapa means lid or cover. The first tapas were pieces of bread used to cover wineglasses so that flies would not enter. Today, tapas are appetizers made from a wide assortment of foods. They can be small bites of food or miniversions of regular dishes. A typical tapas bar might serve thirty or more kinds, ranging from mushrooms in garlic sauce to octopus in paprika sauce to pigs' feet in tomato, olive oil, onion, and garlic sauce.

One of the pleasures of going out for tapas is to explore new tapas bars. The custom is to go on a *chateo*, or tour of bars, tasting tapas and sherry at each. It is not unusual for a person to satisfy one's appetite this way and skip the evening meal altogether.

The tapas pictured here include olives, shrimp, roasted peppers, pistachios, fish, and calamari.

PRIMARY AND SECONDARY EDUCATION

From the Middle Ages through the middle of the twentieth century, the Catholic Church played a dominant role in education in Spain. The public school system was not established until the mid-1800s, with the Moyano Law of 1857. Until the 1960s, Spain lagged far behind most other European nations in this vital area. Since then, particularly when the General Law on Education was passed in the 1970s, changes in the system have enabled Spanish schools to make great strides. When the autonomous communities were created, some control over education was passed to the regional governments. In this way, the Catalan and Basque languages were made mandatory subjects in local regions where they previously had not been taught at all.

Although primary education is free, demand has exceeded available public facilities and teachers have been in short supply. Increased government subsidies to private schools have allowed them to accept more students for free or at a reduced rate. Today, about one out of every three primary school students attends a private school, the great majority of which are run by the Catholic Church. The rate of illiteracy has dropped to approximately 3 percent. Secondary school attendance, especially by women, has increased even more dramatically. An estimated 90 percent of all Spanish youths, including females, now attend secondary school.

Preprimary school is available as an option for children ages three to five. Eight years of compulsory attendance in state-run schools begins at age six. Five years in primary school is followed by three years in secondary school. At that time, students may opt to enter a three-year *bachillerato* program (Bachillerato Unificado Polivalente—BUP). Those who go on must take a one-year college orientation program (Curso de Orientación—COU) to prepare them for acceptance into the universities. Students who do not wish to attend a university may instead take a vocational training course for either one or two years.

POSTSECONDARY EDUCATION

As much as primary and secondary education has grown since the 1960s, education in the universities has made even greater strides. Prior to the 1960s, only the children of middle- or upper-class families had the opportunity to attend postsecondary institutions. By the late 1980s, Spain had the second-highest percentage of university students to population in all the countries of Western Europe.

The university system is divided into three cycles. The first, leading to the equivalent of a bachelor's degree *(diplomado)*, lasts for three years. The second cycle, comparable to

Converted into a library, a sixteenth-century building at the University of Barcelona serves as a study place for many students.

a master's degree *(licenciado),* lasts for either two or three years. The final cycle, leading to a doctorate *(doctorado),* requires another two years of study and the submission of a thesis.

Among the better-known universities, in order of their establishment, are the University of Salamanca (1218), the University of Barcelona (1450), the University of Seville (1502), the University of Valencia (1510), the University of Granada (1526), the University of Madrid (1836), and the Polytechnical University of Madrid (1971).

RELIGION

With the completion of the Reconquest in 1492, King Ferdinand and Queen Isabella undertook the mission of the religious purification of Spain. The Inquisition was the means used to reach that goal until it was outlawed in 1834. Shortly thereafter, in 1851, Catholicism became the state religion. In 1931, the constitution of the Second Republic decreased the church's power. This encouraged the church to support the Nationalist movement of Francisco Franco five years later.

Franco restored some of the the church's privileges, but change was in the air. In 1965, the Second Vatican Council endorsed the separation of church and state. The 1978 constitution attempted to further reduce the Catholic Church's influence by denying its status as the state religion. Complete religious freedom was granted to all, but the church's role in Spanish society was also acknowledged.

That role remains an important one, as approximately 95 percent of the population is Roman Catholic. Another 1 percent is Muslim, while 4 percent are members of other religions. Although the great majority of citizens are Catholic, the percentage who attend church regularly has dropped markedly since the 1950s and now stands at about 20 percent.

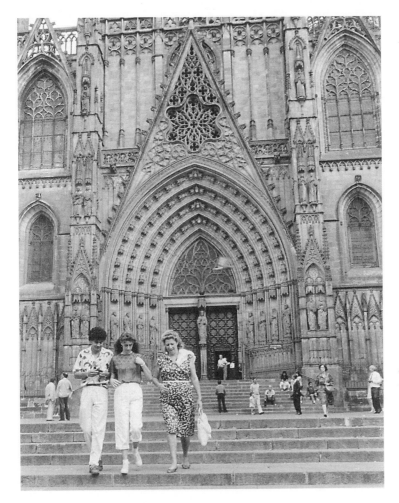

A family leaves Barcelona Gothic Cathedral. Although church attendance has dropped sharply in recent years, most Spaniards identify themselves as Roman Catholic.

Practically all Spaniards, however, celebrate the major church rites, such as baptism, first communion, and marriage. The seeds of the current disaffection with the church were likely planted during the Civil War, when the church represented repression and a return to the old order. Other factors include the higher standard of living and more materialistic outlook on the part of most Spaniards and the migration of many people from rural areas to the cities. Another gauge of the increasingly secular mood in Spanish society is the reduced number of people entering religious orders and becoming priests.

SOCIAL SERVICES

Spain has a widespread system of social welfare programs that provide financial benefits to those in need. Most of these programs, instituted following the reform of the social services in 1978, come under the supervision of the Ministry of Labor and Social Security. The increased prosperity experienced by the country since the mid-1960s has translated into increased government assistance for those who remain in need.

The health care system, administered through the National Institute of Health (part of the Ministry of Health and Consumer Affairs), has been very successful in tending to the medical needs of the populace. The full range of services offered by the system has helped bring about dramatic improvements in the well-being of Spanish citizens. As a result, Spain currently enjoys one of the highest life expectancies of any modern nation.

Other services are offered in addition to health care. The government provides disability payments for those unable to work, pensions for those who are retired, and unemployment insurance for those unable to find work. The benefits are subsidized by a combination of tax proceeds, employer contributions, and deductions from salary. Since the 1980s, the state's share of the funding has expanded greatly. The welfare system at that time was under severe financial stress, due partly to the country's economic adversity.

A move to further enhance the financial level of retired persons and the unemployed has been underway in recent decades. New policies have also been implemented to protect the rights of women and children.

SAN FERMÍN FESTIVAL

Mention the name Pamplona to most people and the picture that comes to mind is dozens of young men, dressed in white, running through narrow, cobblestone streets with enraged bulls hot on their tails. Indeed, the *encierro,* or "running of the bulls," is the most famous event of the San Fermín festival held in Navarre each July. The tradition dates back to 1591, probably beginning as a way for boys to impress girls with their bravery. A description of the event appeared in Ernest Hemingway's *The Sun Also Rises* (1926), giving a boost to its popularity.

This, however, is just one of the many activities that take place during the nine-day-long celebration honoring the city's first bishop. Bullfights, jai alai matches, and singing contests also draw spectators, as do the fireworks that light up the night skies. The festival is a nonstop marathon of drinking and partying.

In the eyes of many, the running of the bulls—which has claimed more than a dozen lives this century—is not even the most dangerous event of the festival. That honor goes to the tradition of monument jumping.

When the opening ceremonies are completed on July 6, many people head to the Mussell Bar in Pamplona Plaza to continue the merrymaking. Outside the bar, in the middle of the plaza, stands a twenty-foot-high monument. Those who have had more than just a little bit to drink climb to the top of the statue. From there, they leap headlong into a stretcher of human hands rising up beneath them. Although there are more than enough people in the plaza to break the jumper's fall, it is important to remember that the major-ity are no more sober than the jumper is. It is no won-der that many who plunge to the cobblestone street, usu-ally littered with broken glass, end up breaking more than their fall.

The running of the bulls in Navarre.

TRANSPORTATION

In a country where miles and miles of harsh, demanding terrain separate the small villages and hamlets that dot the countryside, it is not surprising that the transportation system has much room for improvement. A network of highways emanates from Madrid, the capital and center of the country, while others run along the coast to connect the main coastal cities. Much of the interior, however, remains joined by roads in serious need of upgrading.

Traffic in some of the major cities can be unbearable, due in part to the practice of closing businesses for the three-hour midday siesta. Many people go home at this time and return to work later. This means drivers have four rush hours to contend with rather than two.

Railroad construction began in Spain in the mid-1800s, and the first line, between Madrid and Mataró, was completed in 1848. Many small railroad companies were nationalized during Franco's regime and united under the Spanish National Railroad Network (*Red Nacional de los Ferrocarriles Españoles—* RENFE) in 1941. Unfortunately, the state-owned railroads ran on a narrower-gauge track than that used in systems in neighboring countries. Travelers had to disembark and change trains at the French border. This problem has been corrected, in part, with the introduction of the Talgo, a modern train that runs from Madrid to Paris. The Talgo can adjust the width of

Barcelona, the second largest city in Spain, is a major transportation center.

its axles as it crosses the border, making a change of trains unnecessary.

There are forty-two airports in Spain that receive commercial traffic. Many of these can accommodate international flights. The most heavily trafficked are in the major cities, Madrid (Barajas Airport) and Barcelona, and in tourist regions like Palma de Mallorca in the Baleares. Iberia, the largest Spanish airline, is government owned.

Spain's rivers, with the exception of the Guadalquivir, are of minor economic importance. There are many excellent ports along the coastlines, however, which can accommodate both passenger and freight cargoes. Among the most important ports and harbors are Áviles, Algeciras, Barcelona, Bilbao, Cádiz, Cartagena, Huelva, Las Palmas, Málaga, Gijón, Santa Cruz de Tenerife, Santander, Tarragona, Ceuta, Valencia, and Vigo.

Two girls read Barcelona's La Vanguardia, *one of some ninety newspapers published daily in Spain.*

COMMUNICATIONS

Only in relatively recent times has Spain experienced freedom of the press. Censorship prevailed during Franco's rule, when only progovernment news was disseminated to the general public. The 1978 constitution guaranteed freedom of expression, and the number of periodicals published quickly multiplied. Currently, some ninety newspapers are published daily. The largest and most influential of these is El País, which was founded in Madrid in 1976. Barcelona's La Vanguardia is another influential daily. A number of weekly and monthly magazines are also successful, particularly ones dealing with celebrities and gossip.

When introduced to the country in 1956, all television broadcasting was regulated by the government, and only two channels were available. Both were controlled by the state monopoly, *Radio-Televisión Española* (RTVE). In 1989, the Socialist government allowed private networks to operate. Today, television programming is much like it is in the United States, including sitcoms, game shows, movies, sports, and soap operas.

Radio broadcasting made its first appearance in the 1920s. *Radio Nacional Española* was established by the government during the Civil War, but government control was never as tight as it was for television. By the 1980s, numerous privately owned radio stations were in operation.

THE SOUL OF SPAIN

Spain possesses an extraordinarily rich cultural heritage, as grand as that of virtually any country in the world. The exuberance of the Spanish spirit is revealed in the way the people celebrate their holidays, construct their buildings, dance to their music, and express themselves on both paper and canvas.

The soul of Spain can be discovered in the legacies of the civilizations that have made the Iberian Peninsula their home over the centuries. Each one has added its unique character to the blend that has emerged over hundreds of years. A common thread, however, dating back nearly two thousand years, has been the influence of the Catholic Church. One must fully comprehend the overwhelming importance of this component in order to truly understand the soul of Spain.

HOLIDAYS AND FESTIVALS

Since Spain's population is overwhelmingly Catholic, it is understandable that most holidays are religious in origin. Epiphany, Maundy (or Holy) Thursday, Good Friday, Easter Monday, Corpus Christi, Santiago de Compostela's Day (the Feast of Saint James), and All Saints' Day are the most important national celebrations. October 12 is celebrated as the Day of the Virgin of El Pilar, as well as the civic holiday recognizing the discovery of America by Christopher Columbus.

Nonreligious holidays include New Year's Day and Constitution Day, which has been an official national holiday since 1978. The day on which the Spanish Civil War began (July 18) was originally designated as a national holiday, but this holiday has not been observed since the death of Francisco Franco.

63

Many of Spain's holidays and celebrations, including this Holy Week procession in Andalusia, reflect the country's large Catholic population.

Additional regional holidays are celebrated in Catalonia and the Basque Country, and many villages and towns have their own fiestas. Local festivals of this type often honor a local patron saint or religious miracle and are commonly observed in summer or fall, following the harvest. These celebrations are denoted by the townspeople dressing in colorful costumes and reveling in the music, crafts, and food of the region. Among the more famous of these festivals are the *fallas de Valencia,* which is part of *Semana Santa,* or Holy Week, and the Fiesta of San Fermín in Pamplona, accompanied by the "running of the bulls."

ART AND ARCHITECTURE

The arts hold a prominent position in the heritage of Spain. Each of the cultures that have occupied the Iberian Peninsula through the centuries has added its own imprint on the country's artistic legacy. The cave paintings at Altamira are the earliest examples that survive from prehistoric days. The stone bust known as *The Lady of Elche* attests to the skills of the fifth century B.C. Iberian artisans.

ANTONIO GAUDÍ AND LA SAGRADA FAMILIA

Antonio Gaudí y Cornet was one of the most imaginative, creative, and original architects of modern times. The son of a coppersmith, he was born in Reus, in Catalonia, in 1852. After graduating from the Provincial School of Architecture in Barcelona, he developed his own signature technique after experimenting with Victorian, Mudéjar (a mixture of Muslim and Christian), Gothic, and Baroque styles.

Gaudí used forms and textures to give his works the look of objects in total harmony with nature's laws. Some structures, for example, are equilibrated, which means they stand without internal columns or external support, as a tree stands.

In 1883, Gaudí was appointed as the official architect of La Sagrada Familia, or the Expiatory Temple of the Holy Family, in Barcelona. He devoted the rest of his life to the project, though it would be only one-quarter completed when he was struck and killed by a trolley car in 1926.

The Gothic-style Expiatory Temple cathedral is a complex structure of singular design, as evidenced by the four towering open-worked spires of the entrance facade and the art noveau stonework. Inspired by the jagged peaks of the nearby mountain of Montserrat, it dominates the Barcelona skyline and attracts more than half a million visitors yearly.

Although most of Gaudí's plans and sketches for the cathedral were destroyed during the Spanish Civil War, other architects have been commissioned to proceed with the construction. Some Spaniards argue that the work should be stopped since it can no longer be considered faithful to Gaudí's original design. Despite being the center of much controversy, however, work continues on the basilica to the present day. If it is ever completed, it will be the tallest church in all of Europe; however, work is projected well into the twenty-first century.

Barcelona's La Sagrada Familia, if ever completed, will be the tallest church in Europe.

Roman influence in art and architecture can be seen throughout Spain. Many Roman structures exist in cities like Barcelona and Tarragona, and an eight-hundred-meter-long brick aqueduct in Segovia is still in use today. The artistic style of the Middle Ages results from a blending of Moorish and Christian cultures. The Alhambra in Granada and the Great Mosque in Córdoba are representative of this era. Churches and monuments of the eleventh, twelfth, and thirteenth centuries were built in the style known as Romanesque. These were followed by the French Gothic structures of the 1400s and 1500s. The dozens of castles that dot the landscape of central Spain are also reminders of these bygone periods.

The Golden Age (1500–1681) saw Spain produce some of its greatest artists, the most famous of whom was the Greek, Doménikos Theotokópoulos, better known as El Greco (1541–1614). Born in Crete, he moved to Toledo as a young man. He is best remembered for his religious scenes, several of which adorn the walls of the Toledo cathedral. El Greco was followed by other artists of distinction, including Diego Rodríguez de Silva Velázquez (1599–1660), Francisco de Zurbarán (1598–1664), and Bartolomé Esteban Murillo (1617–1682). As these painters performed their magic, a Spanish Renaissance style of architecture also evolved. The Escorial, Philip II's palace near Madrid, illustrates this approach. Late in the seventeenth century and early in the eighteenth, architects began to incorporate more imagination into their designs.

The eighteenth-century works of Francisco José de Goya y Lucientes (1746–1828) won acclaim within the European art world. Goya gained fame as one of the most prolific painters of the century and became the official court painter of Carlos III. Later, Antonio Gaudí y Cornet (1852–1926), Spain's greatest modern architect, astonished the art world with his extraordinary organic designs and fabulist sculptures in Barcelona. The unfinished Sagrada Familia cathedral is his most famous work and one of the most recognizable structures in all of Spain.

The modern art movement of the early twentieth century, though emanating from France, had a distinctly Spanish flavor. This period, known as the Silver Age, saw Spain produce some of its most famous masters. Pablo Picasso (1881–1973),

GUGGENHEIM MUSEUM BILBAO

Bilbao is an unspectacular Basque city, once a capital of Spanish industry. One would not expect to find there what *Time* magazine called "the first great building of the 21st century." But find it you will, along the banks of the Nervion River. The building is the exciting Guggenheim Museum Bilbao, which opened on October 19, 1997, "with the force of an architectural meteorite," according to writer Robert Hughes. It is part of an ambitious plan to promote the city as an international cultural center. Whether it succeeds in doing so remains to be seen, but what is certain, however, is that it is one of the most creative pieces of architecture of its time.

Built by American architect Frank O. Gehry, the 250,000-square-foot structure is composed of what appears to be a jumble of interconnected shapes integrated under a shimmering titanium roof—known as the "metallic flower"—which embraces a cluster of meandering, twisting shapes. (Gehry had obtained the costly metal at a discount in 1993 when the Russians started unloading their stockpiles.) At first glance, there does not appear to be a right angle in the entire irregular structure. The exterior also makes use of large expanses of glass, as well as a tall tower dressed in stone.

Upon entering the building, one descends a funnel-shaped grand staircase that leads to a soaring atrium. From here, several galleries branch off, the largest being 450 feet long and known as "the Boat." The immense size of the building allows it to house pieces that are of a grand scale, such as artist Richard Serra's 104-foot-long sculpture *Snake*.

The heart of the Guggenheim Museum Bilbao, topped with a titanium roof, is known as the "metallic flower."

Young Woman Seated in an Arm-Chair *by Pablo Picasso, the man considered by many to be the greatest artist of the twentieth century.*

one of the founders of cubism, is widely considered the greatest artist of the twentieth century and one of the most prolific. Any discussion of modern art has to include mention of the cubist Juan Gris (1887–1927), and surrealists Joan Miró (1893–1983) and Salvador Dalí (1904–1989). Dalí's outrageous paintings and extravagant personality brought him global recognition. Today, a revival of art in Spain has been ignited by the opening of new museums in Madrid, Barcelona, Seville, and Valencia. Among current Spanish artists of note are Antoní Tapiès, Fernando Botero, Pedro Sevilla, Antonio Saura, and Miguel Barceló.

LITERATURE

The literature of Spain dates to the eleventh century. Most of the earliest literature dealt with Christian themes. The first of these works were short lyric poems called *jarchas.* These were followed by the epic poems of the *juglares,* or minstrels, who sang in village squares. The Christians' struggle against the Moors was often the subject of these epics, of which *Cantar del mío Cid* (*Poem of My Cid*) was perhaps the most famous.

The medieval period saw the development of a literature in prose, mostly through the efforts of King Alfonso X, who attempted to compile the collected knowledge of the time. The greatest prose writer of the age was Alfonso's nephew, Don Juan Manuel. The fourteenth century also saw the poetry of Juan Ruiz, the archpriest of Hita, take center stage. His *Libro de buen amor (Book of Good Love)* is one of the masterpieces of Spanish literature.

During the fifteenth century, poets such as Íñigo López de Mendoza, Juan de Mena, and Jorge Manrique come to the fore. The year 1499 is remembered as the year of the *Tragicomedia de Calisto y Melibea (Tragicomedy of Calisto and*

Melibea), better known as *La Celestina*. This novel by Fernando de Rojas ranks among the greatest of Spanish novels.

The Spanish Renaissance and the Golden Age saw Garcilaso de la Vega, Juan Boscán Almogáver, Fernando de Herrera, Juan de Yepes y Álvarez, and Luis de León continue the tradition of Spanish poetry. The early Spanish novel reached its peak during this age with the publication of Miguel de Cervantes Saavedra's (1547–1616) classic, *El ingenioso hidalgo Don Quixote de la Mancha (The History of the Valorous and Witty Knight-Errant, Don Quixote of the Mancha)*. Cervantes's work, regarded as one of the world's great novels, examines the world of chivalry as seen through the eyes of the mad nobleman Don Quixote, who believes himself to be a knight whose calling it is to correct the injustices of the world. Together with his faithful squire Sancho Panza, Don Quixote wanders the countryside, dedicating his accomplishments to his lady, Dulcinea.

Spanish drama also emerged as an important force during this time. Lope de Rueda, Juan de la Cueva de la Garoza, Guillén de Castro y Bellvís, Tirso de Molina, Juan Ruiz de Alarcón Mendoza, and Pedro Calderón de la Barca all made important contributions to the theater. The most prolific of all was Lope Félix de Vega Carpio, who wrote more than one thousand plays and perfected the three-act mixture of comedy and drama known as *comedia.*

As Spain's standing as a world power decreased in the eighteenth century, so, too, did its artistic inspiration. Among the few figures who made significant contributions were the essayist Benito Jerónimo Feijoo y Montenegro and dramatists Leandro Fernández de Moratín and Ramón de la Cruz.

Romanticism pervaded European literature in the nineteenth century. Spain added to the movement through the works of Ángel de Saavedra, José Zorrilla y Moral, José de Espronceda, and Mariano José de Larra. In the second half of the century, romanticism gave way to realism. Novelists known for their depictions of life in the various provinces of Spain include Benito Pérez Galdós, José María de Pereda, Pedro Antonio de Alarcón, Emilia Pardo Bazán, Armando Palacio Valdés, and Vicente Blasco Ibáñez.

At the end of the nineteenth century a group of writers, dedicated to bringing an awareness of the need for modernization to Spain, made their mark on Spanish literature.

These writers, known as "The Generation of 1898," included Miguel de Unamuno, Ramón María del Valle-Inclán, Antonio Machado y Ruiz, Pío Baroja y Nessi, José Martínez Ruiz, and Jacinto Benavente y Martínez. Shortly before the Spanish Civil War, a cluster of poets known as "The Generation of 1927" opened the world of Spanish verse to new ideas. Federico García Lorca, shot and killed at age thirty-six by Franco's Nationalists in the early days of the war, is the most famous of this group, which also includes Jorge Guillén, Rafael Alberti, and Vicente Aleixandre y Merlo.

Since that time, Miguel Hernández, Germán Bleiberg, Rafael Morales, Blas de Otero, Lorenzo Gomís, Javier Salvago, and José Hierro have all had an impact on contemporary poetry. Recent novelists of note include Juan Antonio de Zunzunegui, Max Aub, Francisco Ayala, Ignacio Agusti, Rafael Sánchez Ferlosio, Eduardo Mendoza, Luis Goytisolo, Montserrat Roig, Carmen Laforet, and Ramón Sender, while a list of the best contemporary playwrights would have to contain the names of Antonio Buero Vallejo, Alfonso Paso, and Alfonso Sastre. The past thirty years have also witnessed the emergence of several important women writers, including Adelaida García Morales and Ana María Matute. Spanish authors who have collected Nobel Prizes for their work include dramatists José Echegaray (1904) and Jacinto Benavente (1922), poets Juan Ramón Jiménez (1956) and Vicente Aleixandre y Merlo (1977), and novelist Camilo José Cela (1989).

MUSIC AND DANCE

The foundations of Spanish music can be traced back to the time when the Moors controlled the peninsula. The style called *cante jondo* ("deep song") was developed and popularized in the southern region of Andalusia. When Ferdinand and Isabella united Spain in 1492, it signaled the beginning of a period in which the arts would thrive. Each region of the country added its own variations to the music that developed. The heroic exploits of the Christians who drove out the Moors became common themes for ballads of the day.

By the sixteenth and seventeenth centuries, pieces for the *vihuela* (similar to the lute) and guitar were being written by such composers as Luis de Milan, Enriquez de Valderabano, Esteban Daza, and Miguel de Fuenllana. Other composers, like Tomás Luis de Victoria, Cristobal de Morales, and Francisco Guerrero, concentrated on writing church music. The seventeenth century marked the birth of the opera in Spain. Soon, however, opera was surpassed in popularity by the zarzuela, which combined musical plays with song, dance, and spoken excerpts. This form reached its height in the nineteenth century, with Francisco Asenjo Barbieri as its foremost practitioner.

The onset of the twentieth century witnessed the emergence to prominence of composers Isaac Albéniz, Enrique Granados, and Joaquín Turina, whose music reflected the rich heritage of the various provinces of Spain. The ballets of Manuel de Falla brought him worldwide fame in the early decades of the century. In more recent years, Joaquin Rodrigo, Federico Mompou, Rodolfo Halffter, Joaquin Homs, Cristobal Halffter, Roberto Gerhard, and Luis de Pablo have continued to perpetuate the Spanish tradition of vitality and rhythm in their music.

Violinist Yehudi Menuhin accompanies Montserrat Caballé, who is recognized as one of the great opera singers of the twentieth century.

In addition to its composers, Spain has also graced the world with its share of talented performers. Plácido Domingo, José Carreras, and Montserrat Caballé are among the greatest opera singers on the world stage. The country that has given the world the guitar, tambourine, castanets, and *gaita* (a kind of bagpipe) has also produced its share of great instrumentalists, including guitarists Andrés Segovia and Narciso Yepes, cellist Pablo Casals, and pianist Alicia de Larrocha.

Contemporary genres such as pop, rock, and jazz are popular with the younger generation of Spaniards. Singer Julio Iglesias has become known internationally through his concert appearances.

ANDRÉS SEGOVIA

The popularity of the guitar as a major instrument in Spanish classical music is due mainly to the efforts and talent of one man—Andrés Segovia. Segovia was born in Linares, Andalusia, on February 21, 1893. As a boy, he studied piano, violin, and cello, but his real love was the guitar. Since the instrument was held in low esteem at the time and not deemed worthy of serious study, Segovia taught himself, against the wishes of his parents, who felt his talent was being wasted. His prowess was noteworthy, however, and he made his professional debut in 1909 while still a teenage student at the Granada Musical Institute. He became well known locally but did not forge a reputation internationally until a 1924 concert in Paris.

Segovia himself transcribed for the guitar more than 150 works originally written for other instruments. His genius inspired twentieth-century composers like Mario Castelnuovo-Tedesco, Alfredo Casella, Manuel de Falla, Francis Poulenc, and Albert Roussel to write pieces specifically for the guitar. Among the honors he was awarded were the Grand Cross of Isabel la Católica, the Royal Philharmonic Society Gold Medal, the Japanese Order of the Rising Sun, and the Grand Cross of the Order of Merit of the Italian Republic. At the time of his death in 1987, Segovia was universally acclaimed as the leading guitarist of his time.

During his long career, Andrés Segovia brought the classical guitar into the mainstream of the music world.

The roots of modern Spanish dance reach back through the centuries. Each region of the country developed its own characteristic folk music and dances. Among these regional dances are the *jota* of Aragón, the *sardana* of Catalonia, the *sevillanas* of Andalusia, and the flamenco of the Gypsies of southern Spain. Other dances include the fandango, *zarabanda*, seguidilla, and the bolero, which is considered the national dance of Spain.

The bolero, introduced to Spain in the late 1700s, features dancers using graceful hand and arm movements to accompany the complicated steps, performed in syncopated rhythm. Maurice Ravel's *Boléro* is a famous example of the bolero in classical form.

THE CINEMA

As a result of censorship during Franco's authoritarian regime, Spain's motion picture industry developed at a much slower rate than in other Western European countries. Due to Franco's tyrannical administration, the man generally acknowledged as the greatest Spanish director of all time, Luis Buñuel, produced most of his films outside of his homeland.

Not until the 1950s did the work of Juan Antonio Bardem and Luis García Berlanga begin to gain recognition. Modern directors like Pedro Almodóvar (known for his madcap farces), Carlos Saura, Pilar Miró, and Victor Erice have made names for themselves in recent years, both in Spain and internationally. Generally, however, Spanish movies have not gained international acclaim except in rare cases, such as with *Begin the Beguine,* which won an Oscar for José Luis Garci as the Best Foreign Film of 1982.

A flamenco dancer performs on a Barcelona street. Flamenco originated in India and was brought to Spain by trained performers of the Moorish courts.

SPORTS

Until relatively recently, bullfighting was by far the most popular spectator sport in Spain. Soccer *(fútbol),* however, has now taken over the top spot, as it has in most countries of the world. Introduced into Spain by the British in the late 1800s, soccer surpassed bullfighting by the 1950s. Today, thousands of fans follow their local and regional teams with a passionate devotion. The famous Real Madrid squad is one of Europe's best professional clubs.

Interest in basketball has grown immensely since Spain won the silver medal in the 1984 Summer Olympics in Los Angeles. The country's professional basketball league—*Asociación de Clubes de Baloncesto* (ACB)—fields eighteen

The 1992 Summer Olympics brought world recognition to Spanish athletes and to Barcelona.

teams across the country. Fans also follow American basketball on television. American-style football likewise has fans in Spain, where the Barcelona Dragons are one of the teams in the NFL Europe League, formerly known as the World League. The Dragons were crowned champions in 1997 after winning the league's World Bowl.

Another favorite pastime is the Basque sport of *pelota vasca,* better known as jai alai ("merry festival"). Called the "fastest game in the world," jai alai is played on a three-walled concrete court, or fronton. The players use curved wicker baskets, called cestas, to catch a hard rubber ball, which is flung against the wall at speeds of more than one hundred miles per hour.

Tennis players Arantxa Sánchez Vicario and Sergi Bruguera, cyclists Miguel Indurain and Pedro Delgado, soccer player Emilio Buitragueño, and golfers José María Olazábal and Severiano Ballesteros are native Spaniards known to fans of their sports throughout the world. When Barcelona played host to the Summer Olympics in 1992, it gave numerous other Spanish athletes a chance to excel on the world stage. Cyclist José Manuel Moreno, judoists Miriam Blasco and Almudena Múñoz, swimmer Martin Lopez Zubero, and track stars Fermín Cacho, and Daniel Plaza Montero all distinguished themselves with medal-winning efforts. Spain finished eighth in the standings, with thirteen gold medals and twenty-two medals overall, in what Olympic historian John MacAloon called "a public, popular festival, the most extraordinary Olympics I've ever been associated with."[5]

LA CORRIDA

The French writer and educator Jacques Barzun once wrote, "Whoever would understand the heart and mind of America had better learn baseball."[6] Likewise, to understand the heart and mind of Spain, one had better learn *la corrida,* or "the bullfight." Despite pressure applied by international animal rights activists, it continues to be an extremely popular spectacle and has experienced a revitalization in recent years.

Outwardly, the bullfight, known as *la fiesta brava* ("the brave festival") or *la corrida de toros* ("the running of the bulls"), is a struggle between man and bull. Many outsiders find this confrontation to be brutal, cruel, and unnecessary.

A matador at the Plaza de Toros *in Madrid engages a bull, already weakened by its encounters with the picadores and banderilleros, in the final, fatal phase of the fight.*

In reality, it is a struggle between the matador and himself. In no way is the event a fight or sport. Rather, it is a display by which man attempts to demonstrate his dominance over the strongest and bravest that the animal kingdom has to offer—a bull specifically bred for aggressive behavior and instincts.

Existing in some form since ancient times, the modern bullfight has remained relatively unchanged since 1726. Prior to that, it was performed by members of the aristocracy on horseback. Despite occasional efforts to prohibit it, it has remained a fiesta for the masses. Variations of bullfighting styles and strategies can be found in Portugal, southern France, and Latin America. In Portugal, for example, the major participants fight from horseback and never kill the bull.

An afternoon's corrida consists of six bulls to be killed by three matadors. Each encounter consists of three main parts, or *tercios*. At exactly five o'clock, the matadors enter the ring in their ornate costumes, followed by their cuadrillas, or assistants. After the first bull is released, the matador makes a brief series of passes with a red cape. The success of the matador is judged by how close he comes to the bull's horns, his calmness in the face of danger, and the grace of his moves with the cape. The bull is actually attracted by the movement of the cape waved at him, rather than by its color.

After the initial series of passes, the next part commences. Two picadores on horseback attack the bull with short poles or lances in order to wound and weaken him. Next, the banderilleros stick barbed darts (banderillas) in the animal's shoulders or neck. The matador now faces the weakened bull in the *tercio de muerte,* or death phase of the event. The final series of passes is made, with the matador working his way closer and closer to the animal's horns. It is now time for the kill. The matador takes his sword and attempts to slip the blade between the bull's shoulder blades into a small indentation, ringed by bone, which leads to the aorta. It is the "moment of truth" that the crowd and the matador have both been awaiting. Depending on the matador's skill, bravery, and grace, the judge will award him one or two of the bull's ears for a clean kill and occasionally the tail or even a hoof. In times past, this meant he could claim the animal's carcass to sell for meat.

The greatest matadors are treated as superstars by the adoring public. They may earn as much as the equivalent of $25,000 per corrida. The names of immortals such as Juan Belmonte, El Cordobés, and Manolete are revered throughout the bullfighting world.

5

INTO THE TWENTY-FIRST CENTURY

As a developing nation, Spain has been subjected to many critical changes and modifications over the course of the past hundred years. Dictatorships have risen and fallen, and democracy has emerged from the ruins. Isolationism has given way to full membership in the European—and world—community. Wars have been fought, both in other countries and on Spanish soil. Enemies have become allies, and vice versa. A number of pressing issues demand the attention of Juan Carlos's government as it considers the path Spain will take in the twenty-first century.

GOVERNMENT

The government facing these future issues is a parliamentary monarchy, functioning under a constitution that was ratified in 1978. Juan Carlos I has been king since the death of Francisco Franco in 1975, having been designated as the dictator's successor by Franco himself in 1969. Although he is Spain's head of state, the king acts only as an adviser to the prime minister and as commander in chief of the armed forces. He also represents the nation in international affairs.

The king recommends the appointment of the prime minister after conferring with members of the majority party. If the candidate receives a majority of votes from the Congress of Deputies, he is then appointed. José María Aznar López has been Spain's prime minister since May 5, 1996. Other members of the Council of Ministers (or cabinet) are appointed at the suggestion of the prime minister.

The legislature, known as the General Courts (Cortes Generales), consists of the Congress of Deputies (Congreso de los Diputados) with 350 members and the Senate (Senado) with

JOSÉ MARÍA AZNAR LÓPEZ

José María Aznar López, the leader of the Popular Party (PP), became the new prime minister of Spain on May 5, 1996, after his appointment was approved by the Spanish Cortes. He replaced Felipe González Márquez and brought an end to fourteen years of Socialist Party rule.

Aznar, a former tax inspector, was brought up in a conservative household, both his father and grandfather having held government jobs during Franco's regime. Aznar became an active member of the Popular Alliance (the PP's predecessor) and began to advocate a more moderate path of action. When Manuel Fraga Iribarne retired in 1989, Aznar took over leadership of the party as an elected member of the Cortes from Madrid.

News of scandals in González's Socialist Party government allowed the Popular Party to pick up seats in the 1995 elections. Since the PP fell short of a legislative majority in the elections, Aznar found it necessary to win the backing of several smaller parties. Despite these problems, he has vowed to continue striving to meet his goals of eliminating corruption in the government and leading Spain into the twenty-first century as a significant figure in the European economic marketplace.

Aznar and his wife, Ana Botella, rejoice after winning Spain's general elections.

more than 250 members. All are elected—by citizens eighteen years of age and older—or appointed to four-year terms of office.

A General Council (Consejo General) composed of lawyers and judges oversees the judicial branch of the government. The highest court in the land is the Supreme Court of Justice, which rules on all cases except those concerning questions of constitutional law. These are decided by a special Constitutional Court. There are seventeen territorial high courts (one for each autonomous community) that try criminal cases. In addition, there are fifty-two provincial high courts and numerous lower courts (such as courts of first instance, courts of judicial proceedings, penal courts, and municipal courts) that handle other matters.

Spain's fifty provinces are grouped into seventeen autonomous communities. Each of these communities has its own regional parliamentary government that resolves local issues, and each province has its own legislature and governor. Citizens vote for the local assemblies, but the national government appoints the provincial governors. Below the community governments lie two additional levels—the fifty provinces and more than eight thousand municipalities.

GIBRALTAR

Gibraltar is a British colony that occupies a narrow limestone peninsula at the southern tip of Spain's Mediterranean coast. This heavily protected air and naval base guards the Strait of Gibraltar, the only point at which the Mediterranean Sea can be accessed from the Atlantic Ocean. As such, it has been of strategic importance through the centuries. (The Coat of Arms of Gibraltar, in fact, includes a depiction of a key as a reminder of its "key" location.) Gibraltar's status as a British colony has been a major point of contention between England and Spain for many years.

The 1,380-foot tall "Rock" was known to the ancients as one of the two Pillars of Hercules (with Mount Hacho on the African coast) that guarded this gateway between two great bodies of water, the Mediterranean and the Atlantic. Following the Reconquest, Gibraltar was wrested from the Moors by Spain and remained in Spanish possession until the eighteenth century. In 1704, Sir George Rooke captured Gibraltar for the British during the War of the Spanish Succession. It was eventually ceded to Britain under the terms of the Treaty of Utrecht, which ended the war in 1713.

Spain twice tried to reconquer Gibraltar, once in 1727, and in the "Great Siege," which lasted from 1779 to 1783. Both attempts proved futile, however, and the peninsula formally became a British colony in 1830. The colony's reputation as a fortress grew, and a civilian community grew up within its walls. Its significance as a strategic naval base was demonstrated in both world wars.

Through the years, Spain has persisted in trying to regain Gibraltar from the British on both geographical and historical grounds. Franco's determination to recover the "Rock" was so great that he closed the frontier between Spain and Gibraltar in 1969. The Spanish side was not reopened until sixteen years later.

Britain, for its part, has granted Gibraltar full internal self-government. The residents of the colony—of mixed Genoese, British, Spanish, Maltese, and Portuguese descent—consider themselves Gibraltarians. When a 1967 referendum presented a choice of returning to Spanish rule or retaining the status quo, the resulting vote was decidedly pro-British.

A woman in La Linea looks out at the Rock of Gibraltar. Its location at the mouth of the Mediterranean has long made it a site of military importance.

Spain, however, argues that the territory was taken from her in wartime and that Spanish citizens were gradually pushed out as it was repopulated with British subjects. Spain continues to pursue its claim to Gibraltar to the present day, but no solution agreeable to both sides has yet been reached.

BASQUE SEPARATISM AND THE ETA

The Basque Country is one section of Spain whose inhabitants have had difficulty committing to the ideal of a unified Spanish nation. Consisting of the three provinces of Vizcaya, Guipúzcoa, and Álava, the region has been one of the most dangerous corners of Europe over the past forty years.

In 1959, extremist members of the Basque Nationalist Party (*Partido Nacionalista Vasco*—PNV) grew frustrated by Franco's attempt to centralize the Spanish government in Madrid. Hoping to achieve this aim, Franco forbade the practice of many Basque customs and traditions and outlawed the teaching of the Basque language in schools. The radical members of PNV urged the use of armed force in fighting back. These militants separated themselves from the PNV and founded Freedom for the Basque Homeland (*Euskadi ta Askatasuna*—ETA). Driven by intense nationalistic

In Madrid, crowds gather in stunned reaction to the violence of ETA terrorism.

pride in its community, the ETA quickly became known for its use of violence in promoting the cause of Basque independence. Although some of its leaders were arrested in the late 1960s, the group survived.

Franco's death in 1975 and the establishment of a democratic government willing to allow regional autonomy for the provinces were not enough to satisfy the ETA. Its members wanted nothing less than complete independence from Spain and used bombings and assassinations, particularly against government officials, security forces, and military personnel, as tools to emphasize their demands. These activities were financed by kidnappings, robberies, and extortion. In response, a government-sponsored death squad killed twenty-seven people in an unlawful attempt to crush the terrorist group in the 1980s. The ETA managed to survive, however, and remained active into the 1990s. Today, more than eight hundred people have lost their lives through ETA violence.

As sympathy for the terrorists declined even among the Basques, the ETA announced an indefinite cease-fire in September 1998. While assassinations have ended, firebombings of property have continued. Many Basques believe that the territory's status as an autonomous community permits enough freedom from the central government in Madrid. However, ending the ETA's campaign of terrorism in its bid for total Basque independence remains a continuing problem for the nation as the new millennium begins.

SPAIN–UNITED STATES RELATIONS

The Spanish-American War of 1898 understandably left most Spaniards with bitter feelings toward the United States. Over the past hundred years, officials on both sides have worked to improve relations between the nations.

A series of trade agreements in the first decade of the twentieth century improved commercial ties between the countries. Spain's economy benefited as manufactured goods and agricultural products changed hands and tourism increased. The Spanish Civil War aroused emotions in the United States, and volunteers traveled to Spain to fight the forces of fascism. With Franco's victory, however, Spain's ties with Germany and Italy chilled relations with the United States. Even though the 1953 Pact of Madrid was a step toward easing ill feelings, anti-Americanism was still strong in Franco's government.

When Juan Carlos became king, significant advances began to occur. The United States welcomed the new democratic government and entered into a Treaty of Friendship and Cooperation in 1976. U.S. military rights in the peninsula were renewed, and the stage was set for Spain to eventually be accepted into NATO. The policies regarding economic aid in exchange for U.S. military base rights have been amended over the years. A 1989 agreement on defense cooperation between the two countries authorized a reduced U.S. presence at Spanish military installations.

The United States and Spain have become more closely associated in recent years. On the scientific front, space tracking stations near Madrid are jointly operated by the U.S. National Aeronautic and Space Administration (NASA) and the Spanish National Aerospace Institute (INTA). Cultural and educational cooperation has also been upgraded through the administration of the binational Fulbright program for graduate students and visiting professors. The cooperative atmosphere between the nations has been secured through visits to each other's land by heads of government, including President Clinton, King Juan Carlos, and Prime Minister Aznar.

SPAIN–LATIN AMERICA RELATIONS

An influential role for Spain in Latin American affairs continues to be a Spanish foreign policy goal, spurred by the shared cultural, linguistic, and religious heritage of the two regions.

Prior to the Spanish-American War, relations between Spain and Latin America had been poor since the age of Spanish imperialism. The war, however, united both regions in their disdain for the United States. Common bonds were emphasized and differences downplayed. As Spain's economy blossomed in the second half of the twentieth century, trade between the Hispanic regions increased.

Following Franco's death in 1975, as Spain grew as a democratic nation, more attention was focused on Latin America. Spanish investment in the area increased significantly, and in 1985, a special assistance program was created. Spain took an active role in recent years in trying to elicit peace during the bloody uprisings in El Salvador, Guatemala, and Nicaragua. Because of the region's Hispanic legacy, such involvement is likely to continue in the foreseeable future.

THE ENVIRONMENT

In Spain, as in every other nation in the modern world, preservation of the environment is a growing concern. Spain is a relative newcomer to the industrialized world community, so it is not surprising that the country lags behind most other nations of Western Europe in environmental regulation. Several incidents in recent years have served to increase public awareness about ecological problems. A succession of oil spills in local waters has threatened the coastal

VANDELLÒS-1

Spain has virtually no petroleum reserves, so the search for alternative sources of energy is a major concern. In 1951 the government of General Francisco Franco created the *Junta de Energía Nuclear* (JEN) as a research and development body to explore the ways nuclear power could benefit the nation. Seventeen years later, the country's first nuclear power plant went on line. Within twenty-five years, eight more plants began operation.

An accident at one of these plants, however, dealt the program a serious blow. On Thursday, October 19, 1989, a fire was started by an explosion in one of the turbines at the Vandellòs-1 nuclear reactor in the province of Tarragona. The fire raged for over four hours, in part because the firefighters had never been given the proper training for the possible occurrence of such an event. For example, water instead of foam was sprayed on electrical systems.

Luckily, the incident did not result in any external release of radioactivity, contamination on site, or damage to the reactor core itself. The Spanish newspaper, *El País*, however, reported that the International Atomic Energy Agency had declared it the worst nuclear accident since the breakdown at Chernobyl in Ukraine. (The IAEA later denied this report.)

The accident was enough to rally antinuclear groups to action. Protesters called on the government to shut down the reactor rather than to make repairs. On May 30, 1990—less than eight months after the accident—the government announced that the plant would not return to operation.

environment. The Spanish tanker *Urquiola* exploded after running aground near La Coruña in 1976, dumping oil over 130 miles of beach. Two years later, a Greek-owned tanker spilled 12 million gallons of oil after sinking just 20 miles offshore. A spill from another Greek tanker in the same general area released more than 21 million gallons of crude in 1992.

Another disaster resulted in the loss of more than three hundred lives in 1981. The deaths were caused by "toxic oil syndrome" (TOS), apparently spread when rapeseed oil, intended for industrial use, was marketed as olive oil. This tragedy illustrated the need for stricter standards in food and drink inspection and regulation.

The government of José María Aznar López, recently established a Ministry of the Environment (*Ministerio de Medio Ambiente*) to address environmental issues. Two of the chief goals of the ministry are the assessment of fines on those responsible for dumping hazardous wastes and seeking ways to recycle toxic materials.

Spain has already experienced a great deal of success in two specific areas—slowing population growth and improving the quality of drinking water. Since the mid-1980s, the nation's population has increased at an average rate of only 0.5 percent annually, compared with rates of more than 3 percent elsewhere. At the same time, Spain's drinking water, which supplies nearly 40 million people, has become 100 percent safe.

In addition to problems native to Spain, the nation must confront other universal problems. Pollution of the Mediterranean by raw sewage and waste products from offshore oil and gas drilling, for example, is a serious problem facing all the nations of the region. Spain has hosted several conferences addressing this and other issues and has signed and ratified numerous international agreements concerning environmental safety and preservation.

THE CHANGING ROLE OF WOMEN

For many centuries, Spanish women held a role in society similar to that of women in other parts of Western Europe and North America. They were considered subordinate to men and did not have equal rights. Their roles were restricted to being wives and mothers. Under Franco's regime, a woman could not take a job without her husband's approval, known as *permiso marital.* Likewise, there was a double standard with regard to moral behavior, with women being held to stricter standards than men and laws concerning adultery and desertion applied differently to women than to men.

Only after Spain became a democracy in the late 1970s did women receive full equality with men under the law. Discrimination on the basis of gender was prohibited beginning with the Constitution of 1978. The number of women entering the workforce increased considerably, even though a high unemployment rate made jobs relatively scarce. While less than one in eight members of the workforce were women in 1910, the current rate is better than one in three.

Women have also taken advantage of the opportunity to better educate themselves. By the 1980s, nearly half of Spain's university admissions were female—one of the highest percentages in the world. With changing times came liberalization of moral values. Laws concerning divorce, contraception, and abortion have all been modified to accommodate women's perspectives.

Despite these gains, work still remains to be done. As the cultural atmosphere of Spain continues to evolve, the role of women will reflect these changes.

Five female scientists walk through the grounds of Madrid's National Science Center. Since passage of a law prohibiting gender discrimination in the late 1970s, women have become an integral part of Spain's work force.

CHANGING VALUES AND ATTITUDES

Spain's transformation from a dictatorship to a democracy brought many profound changes. Conservative values began to collapse as Spaniards had increasing contact with the outside world through increased tourism, the exodus of families from the farms to the cities, and the migration of workers to jobs in other European countries.

With more people working in industry and fewer in agriculture, the standard of living has risen. This, in turn, has caused an increase in consumerism. Increasingly, the modern conveniences taken for granted in the United States have become available to the citizens of Spain. Young people, in particular, have quickly adopted the world of computers, CDs, cars, and telephones. Teenagers follow the latest fashions and music in Spain as they do in other countries of Western Europe. The increased emphasis on material goods has undoubtedly been one of the reasons for the decline in the influence of the church, although the great majority of Spaniards still profess to be Catholics.

These fashion-conscious teens in Old Town, Segovia, reflect the younger generation's increased consumption of material goods.

Unfortunately, technology and social change create negative aspects as well. Greed on the part of government officials has been blamed for large-scale political scandal. The ravages of drug abuse have been felt, particularly in the larger cities. Greater sexual freedom has been accompanied by an increase in the number of unwed mothers. The increased consumption of goods continues to threaten the environment. Although perhaps not as likely to receive front-page headlines as the terrorist acts of the ETA, these problems must nevertheless be addressed if Spain is to become an important player on the world stage.

Every modern nation faces similar problems. An increasingly complex world presents new challenges that must be confronted. The people of Spain look toward the new millenneum with optimism and hope, determined to meet those challenges and to solidify their standing in the world community.

Facts About Spain

Autonomous Communities

Name	Area (sq. mi.)	Population (1994 est.)	Capital
Andalusia	33,822	7,053,043	Seville
Aragón	18,425	1,183,576	Zaragoza
Asturias	4,094	1,083,388	Oviedo
Baleares	1,927	736,865	Palma de Mallorca
Canarias	2,875	1,534,897	Santa Cruz de Tenerife
Cantabria	2,054	526,090	Santander
Castilla–La Mancha	30,680	1,656,179	Toledo
Castilla y León	36,380	2,504,371	Valladolid
Catalonia	12,399	6,090,107	Barcelona
Ceuta	8	68,867	—
Extremadura	16,075	1,050,590	Mérida
Galicia	11,419	2,720,761	Santiago de Compostela
La Rioja	1,948	263,437	Logroño
Madrid	3,100	5,034,548	Madrid
Melilla	5	58,052	—
Murcia	4,368	1,070,401	Murcia
Navarre	4,012	523,614	Pamplona
País Vasco	2,793	2,075,561	Vitoria (Gasteiz)
Valencia	8,979	3,909,047	Valencia
TOTAL	**195,363**	**39,143,394**	

DEMOGRAPHIES

Population (1996): 39,270,000

Population density per square mile (1996): 201.0

Population distribution, urban–rural (1990): urban, 78.4 percent; rural, 21.6 percent

Population distribution by sex (1996): male, 48.93 percent; female, 51.07 percent

Population distribution by age (1996): under 15, 16.2 percent; 15–29, 24.4 percent; 30–44, 21.7 percent; 45–59, 16.6 percent; 60–69, 10.5 percent; 70 and over, 10.6 percent

Population projections (2000): 39,466,000; (2010) 39,917,000

Ethnolinguistic composition (1991): Spanish, 74.4 percent; Catalan, 16.9 percent; Galician, 6.4 percent; Basque, 1.6 percent; other, 0.7 percent

Religious affiliation (1993): Roman Catholic, 94.9 percent; Muslim, 1.2 percent; Protestant, 0.5 percent; other, 3.4 percent

Populations of major cities (1991): Madrid, 3,010,492; Barcelona, 1,641,656; Valencia, 722,856; Seville, 611,364; Zaragoza, 570,541

Birthrate per 1,000 population (1994): 9.3 (world avg. 25.0); (1992) legitimate, 89.5 percent; illegitimate, 10.5 percent

Death rate per 1,000 population (1994): 8.6 (world avg. 9.3)

Natural increase rate per 1,000 population (1994): 0.7 (world avg. 15.7)

Total fertility rate (avg. births per childbearing woman, 1995): 1.3

Marriage rate per 1,000 population (1994): 5.0

Divorce rate per 1,000 population (1990): 0.6

Life expectancy at birth (1995): male, 73.2 years; female, 81.1 years

Major causes of death per 100,000 population (1993): circulatory disease, 343.9; malignant neoplasms (cancers), 219.7; respiratory disease, 81.6

LAND

Land area: 194,884 square miles

Land use (1994): forest, 32.3 percent; meadows and pastures, 21.4 percent; agricultural and under permanent cultivation, 40.3 percent; other, 6.0 percent

Highest point: Pico de Teide, 12,188 feet

ECONOMY

Gross national product (1994): US $525,334,000,000 (US $13,280 per capita)

Budget (1995): Revenue: Ptas [pesetas] 14,077,800,000,000 (direct taxes, 46.1 percent; indirect taxes, 38.9 percent, of which value-added tax on products, 24.9 percent; other taxes on production, 15.0 percent). Expenditures: Ptas 17,326,700,000,000 (public debt, 16.9 percent; health, 14.6 percent; labor and social security, 8.8 percent; education, 6.0 percent; defense, 5.0 percent; pensions, 4.9 percent; interior and justice, 4.6 percent)

Public debt (1995): Ptas 38,697,700,000,000 (US $312,000,000,000)

Household income and expenditures: average household size (1991) 3.4; income per household (1995) Ptas 2,925,116 (US $23,637); sources of income (1991): wages and salaries, 48.5 percent; profits and self-employment, 27.5 percent; social security, 19.5 percent; expenditures (1993): housing, 25.5 percent; food, 23.9 percent; transportation, 13.3 percent; clothing and footwear, 7.7 percent; household goods and services, 6.0 percent

Imports (1995): Ptas 14,318,261,000,000 (machinery, 11.6 percent; energy products, 8.3 percent, of which crude petroleum, 8.2 percent; agricultural products, 7.9 percent; transportation equipment, 7.3 percent)

Major import sources: France, 17.1 percent; Germany, 15.3 percent; Italy, 9.2 percent; U.K., 7.8 percent, Japan, 3.3 percent

Exports: Ptas 11,423,085,000,000 (transport equipment, 20.3 percent; agricultural products, 12.7 percent; machinery, 8.3 percent)

Major export destinations: France, 20.5 percent; Germany, 15.4 percent; Italy, 11.5 percent; U.K., 8.0 percent

Notes

Introduction: A Land of Contrasts

1. John A. Crow, *Spain: The Root and the Flower.* Berkeley and Los Angeles: University of California Press, 1985, p.11.

Chapter 2: Finding a Place in the World Order

2. Quoted in Editors of Time-Life Books, *Spain.* Amsterdam: Time-Life Books, 1986, p. 82.

Chapter 3: A Spectrum of Ethnic Communities

3. Crow, *Spain,* p. 55.

4. Quoted in Adrian Shubert, *The Land and People of Spain.* New York: HarperCollins, 1992, p. 8.

Chapter 4: The Soul of Spain

5. Quoted in Mike Meserole, ed., *The 1993 Information Please Sports Almanac.* Boston: Houghton Mifflin, 1992, p. 556.

6. Quoted in Lee Green, *Sportswit.* New York: Fawcett Crest, 1984, p. 33.

GLOSSARY

alcázar: Moorish palace.

autos-da-fé: Public ceremonies during which the sentences of the Inquisition were carried out.

caudillo: Military leader.

conquistadores: Leaders in the Spanish conquest of the Americas.

convivencia: Spirit of cooperation between cultures in ancient Spain.

fiesta: Celebration.

latifundios: Large plots of farmland.

Madrileños: Citizens of Madrid.

marranos: Persons who converted from Judaism to Christianity.

meseta: The high, dry plateau characteristic of the central part of Spain.

minifundios: Small plots of farmland.

moriscos: Persons who converted from Islam to Christianity.

mosque: Islamic place of worship.

paella: Spanish dish made from meats, seafood, vegetables, and rice.

peseta: Spanish unit of currency.

sangría: Summer drink made from red wine and fruit.

siesta: Midafternoon rest period.

taifa: Small kingdom of the Moors.

tapas: Small portions of varied food served with a drink in a bar.

CHRONOLOGY

B.C.

15,000–12,000
Cave drawings at Altamira painted by prehistoric hunters.

3000
Iberians settle Iberian Peninsula.

1000
Phoenicians arrive from eastern Mediterranea.

900
First wave of Celts settle in northern Spain.

650
Second wave of Celts settle in Spain.

600
Greeks arrive along Mediterranean coast.

400
Carthaginians invade Spain from northern Africa.

228
Barcelona founded by Carthaginians.

205
Romans drive Carthaginians from Spain, adding the peninsula to their empire.

A.D.

ca. 50
Christianity introduced to Spain.

409
Vandals, Suevi, and Alans cross Pyrenees and invade Spain.

411
Visigoths enter Spain.

587
Catholicism adopted as official religion of Spain.

711–716
Moors invade Spain from northern Africa and defeat Visigoths.

722
Pelayo defeats Moors at Covadonga as Christian forces begin Reconquest to gain Spain back from Moors.

1094
El Cid Campeador seizes control of Valencia from Muslims.

1137
Kingdoms of Aragón and Catalonia unite.

1248
Seville falls to Ferdinand of Castile.

1348–1351
Black Death spreads through Europe; nearly one-third of Spain's population succumbs.

1469
Ferdinand, king of Aragón, and Isabella, heir to throne of Castile, marry.

1478
Spanish Inquisition instituted by Pope Sixtus IV.

1479
Kingdoms of Aragón and Castile unite, bringing Spain together under one crown.

1492
Christian troops force Moors from Granada, their final stronghold in Spain, to complete Reconquest; Christopher Columbus claims America for Spain; 150,000 Jews expelled from Spain by royal decree.

1504
Queen Isabella dies.

1512
Ferdinand annexes Navarre, uniting all of what will become modern Spain.

1513
Balboa becomes first European to reach Pacific Ocean.

1516
Charles I becomes first Habsburg to occupy Spanish throne.

1519–1521
Cortés conquers Aztec empire in Mexico.

1522
Magellan leads first expedition to circumnavigate the globe.

1530–1680
Spain's Golden Age of exploration and culture.

1531–1533
Pizarro conquers Incan empire in Peru.

1540
Coronado's expedition sights Grand Canyon and Colorado River; Ignatius Loyola founds Society of Jesus.

1541
De Soto becomes first European to see Mississippi River.

1556
Charles abdicates and is succeeded by son, Philip II.

1561
Philip moves capital to Madrid.

1563–1584
Escorial, the royal palace, built near Madrid.

1564
Spain begins colonization of Philippines.

1568–1648
Protestant dissenters revolt in Netherlands, beginning eighty-year struggle for Dutch independence from Spain.

1577
Cretan painter, El Greco, settles in Toledo.

1588
Spanish Armada defeated by British navy.

1599–1600
Plague kills 500,000 in Castile.

1605
Publication of the first part of Cervantes's *Don Quixote.*

1609–1614
275,000 Moors expelled from Spain.

1621–1700
Decline of Spanish power through series of wars waged by Philip IV and Charles II.

1700
Philip of Anjou becomes King Philip V of Spain, beginning Bourbon rule.

1702–1714
War of Spanish Succession.

1762
Spain enters Seven Years' War as ally of France.

1763
Peace of Paris concludes Seven Years' War.

1767
Jesuits expelled from Spain by Charles III.

1793–1805
France invades Spain, forcing it into alliance against England.

1808
Napoléon places his brother Joseph on Spanish throne, setting off guerrilla war against occupying French forces.

1810–1825
Most Spanish colonies in South America proclaim independence.

1812
Cortes of Cádiz proclaims liberal constitution limiting royal power.

1813
French driven from Spain by combined British, Spanish, and Portuguese forces under Lord Wellington.

1814–1833
Ferdinand VII assumes throne and abrogates constitution.

1833–1839
First Carlist War.

1851
Catholicism becomes state religion of Spain.

1868
Isabella II forced into exile.

1873–1874
Spain governed by First Republic.

1874–1931
Bourbon dynasty restored to Spanish throne.

1898
Spain loses Puerto Rico, Philippine Islands, and Guam to United States as result of Spanish-American War.

1909–1926
Spain attempts to establish protectorate in Morocco.

1917
Socialist-led general strike crushed by military.

1923
General Miguel Primo de Rivera becomes dictator of Spain, with backing of Alfonso XIII.

1930
Primo de Rivera forced to resign.

1931
Spaniards vote for republican form of government; Second Republic established; Alfonso XIII goes into voluntary exile.

1933
Falange Party founded by José Antonio Primo de Rivera.

1936
Popular Front wins decisive majority in general elections.

1936–1939
Spanish Civil War begins; Nationalist forces of General Francisco Franco defeat Loyalists, and Franco becomes dictator.

1937
Bombing of Guernica inspires Picasso's most famous painting.

1939–1945
Spain remains officially neutral in World War II.

1946
United Nations recommends diplomatic and economic boycott of Spain.

1947
Law of Succession is approved, making Spain a monarchy.

1953
Pact of Madrid gives United States right to establish four military bases in Spain in exchange for financial aid.

1955
Spain admitted to United Nations.

1959
Terrorist group ETA founded.

1969
Franco selects Juan Carlos as his successor.

1973
Prime Minister Carrero Blanco assassinated by ETA.

1975
Franco dies; Prince Juan Carlos de Borbón becomes king of Spain.

1976
Law of Political Reform reestablishes democracy in Spain.

1977
First free elections held in forty years.

1978
Spain adopts new democratic Constitution of 1978.

1980
Basque and Catalan parliaments elected.

1981
Juan Carlos helps thwart attempted military coup.

1982

Spain joins NATO; Socialist Party wins control of government through elections.

1983

Formation of Spain's seventeen autonomous communities is completed, ending process of decentralization that began in 1979.

1986

Spain joins European Economic Community (now European Union).

1992

Summer Olympics held in Barcelona; World's Fair in Seville celebrates five hundredth anniversary of Columbus's voyage to New World; Madrid named "Cultural Capital of Europe."

1996

Coalition of conservative and regional parties wins general elections, wresting control from Socialists.

1998

ETA announces first-ever unilateral, indefinite cease-fire in attempt to provoke negotiations with the Spanish government.

Suggestions for Further Reading

Books

Editors of Time-Life Books, *Spain*. Amsterdam: Time-Life Books, 1986. This volume in the Library of Nations series takes a look at the people, land, and history of Spain, with numerous color photographs.

Peter S. Feibleman and the Editors of Time-Life Books, *Cooking of Spain and Portugal*. New York: Time-Life Books, 1970. This volume in the Foods of the World series is a treasure trove of information and recipes dealing with the foods of the Iberian Peninsula.

Norman H. Finkelstein, *The Other 1492*. New York: Beech Tree Books, 1989. A study of the banishment of the Jews from Spain and their eventual settlement in the New World.

Richard Fletcher, *Moorish Spain*. New York: Henry Holt, 1992. An exploration of all areas of Moorish influence in Spain.

Lerner Geography Department, *Spain . . . in Pictures*. Minneapolis: Lerner, 1995. An easy-to-read look at Spain for youngsters, with many photographs.

William W. Lace, *Defeat of the Spanish Armada*. San Diego: Lucent Books, 1997. A clear explanation of the battles that led to the defeat of the Spanish Armada.

Don Lawson, *The Abraham Lincoln Brigade*. New York: Thomas Y. Crowell, 1989. The story of the Americans who traveled to Spain to fight fascism in the Spanish Civil War.

Arthur Miller, *Spain*. Philadelphia: Chelsea House, 1999. An easy-to-read history of Spain; the modern-day nation is also examined.

Adrian Shubert, *The Land and People of Spain.* New York: HarperCollins, 1992. This volume in the Portraits of the Nations series provides an interesting look at the history and traditions of Spain.

Duncan Townson, *Muslim Spain.* Minneapolis: Lerner, 1979. A look at Spain during the Muslim occupation.

WEBSITE

Si, Spain (www.DocuWeb.ca/SiSpain/english/index.html). An interactive service that promotes the free exchange of information on Spanish current affairs and Spain's historical, linguistic, and cultural development.

WORKS CONSULTED

BOOKS

Gerald Brenan, *The Spanish Labyrinth*. London: Cambridge University Press, 1974. A social and political history of the Spanish Civil War.

Raymond Carr, *Spain 1808–1939*. London: Oxford University Press, 1966. A detailed account of the economic, social, and political origins of modern Spain.

Peter N. Carroll, *The Odyssey of the Abraham Lincoln Brigade*. Stanford, CA: Stanford University Press, 1994. This work gives a detailed account of American involvement in the Spanish-American War.

John A. Crow, *Spain: The Root and the Flower*. Berkeley and Los Angeles: University of California Press, 1985. A personal look at Spain and the Spanish people through the eyes of a noted authority on Hispanic culture.

Robert Graham, *Spain: A Nation Comes of Age*. New York: St. Martin's Press, 1984. An examination of modern-day Spain, from Franco to the present.

Lee Green, *Sportswit*. New York: Fawcett Crest, 1984. A collection of quotes concerning all areas of sport.

Robert Hughes, *Barcelona*. New York: Knopf, 1992. A historic look at the city of Barcelona and the Catalan culture it represents.

Juan Lalaguna, *A Traveller's History of Spain*. New York: Interlink Books, 1996. An especially good background history of Spain with more information than can be found in a travel guide.

Mike Meserole, ed., *The 1993 Information Please Sports Almanac*. Boston: Houghton Mifflin, 1992. This annual review of the year in sports also contains listings of records in both major and minor sports.

Rhea Marsh Smith, *Spain*. Ann Arbor: The University of Michigan Press, 1965. A detailed history of Spain, from the time of the first inhabitants up through the dictatorship of Francisco Franco.

Eric Solsten and Sandra W. Meditz, eds., *Spain: A Country Study*. Washington, DC: Federal Research Division, Library of Congress, 1990. A look at government data and information on Spain.

Hugh Thomas, *The Spanish Civil War*. New York: Harper & Row, 1977. A comprehensive analysis of the Spanish Civil War.

Mary Vincent and R. A. Stradling, *Cultural Atlas of Spain & Portugal*. Oxfordshire: Andromeda Oxford Limited, 1994. An examination of the cultural and artistic heritage of the Iberian Peninsula.

Jose Yglesias, *The Franco Years*. New York: Bobbs-Merrill, 1977. An examination of life under Spanish fascism and Francisco Franco.

PERIODICALS

"The Best and Worst of '97 Design," *Time,* December 29, 1997–January 5, 1998, p.132.

Robert Hughes, "Bravo! Bravo!" *Time,* November 3, 1997, p. 104.

INTERNET SOURCE

Leon Lazaroff, "Spanish Civil War volunteers gather for an emotional reunion," *Philadelphia Inquirer,* November 6, 1996. dept.english.upenn.edu/~afilreis/50s/spainreunion.html.

WEBSITES

Gibraltar (www.gibraltar.gi). Website of the British colony of Gibraltar.

Opus Dei (www.opusdei.org/about/inbrief.html). Site of the personal Prelature of the Catholic Church.

INDEX

Picture Credits

ABOUT THE AUTHOR

John F. Grabowski is a native of Brooklyn, New York. He holds a bachelor's degree in psychology from City College of New York and a master's degree in educational psychology from Teacher's College, Columbia University. He has been a teacher for thirty years, as well as a freelance writer specializing in the fields of sports, education, and comedy. His body of published work includes twenty books; a nationally syndicated sports column; consultation on several math textbooks; articles for newspapers, magazines, and the programs of professional sports teams; and comedy material sold to Jay Leno, Joan Rivers, and numerous other comics. He and his wife, Patricia, live in Staten Island with their daughter, Elizabeth.